harbouring
the dream

© Suffolk Yacht Harbour Ltd

Suffolk Yacht Harbour Ltd
Levington Ipswich
Suffolk 1P10 0LN UK

www.syharbour.co.uk

info@syharbour.co.uk

First published 2011

UK ISBN 978-0-9568479-0-4

Designed and edited by
Martin Treadway

Cover aerial photograph by Mike Page

Printed in England by
Fuller Davies Ltd
Baird Close
Hadleigh Road Industrial Estate
Ipswich IP2 OUF

harbouring
the dream

In the 1960s, a small group of sailing enthusiasts transformed 60 acres of flooded marshland into a little harbour for 70 yachts.

By 2011 it had become the most successful marina on the East Coast of England, with outstanding facilities for 550 boats.

Designed and edited by
Martin Treadway

Suffolk Yacht Harbour

Contents

66 The Clubhouse is the ex Trinity Light Vessel LV87

Mike's beautiful 60ft motor yacht, 'Sea Samba', lying on the north side of the East Harbour. She was built by Phillips of Dartmouth in 1964 of Honduras mahogany on oak frames and is powered by two AEC 'London Bus' diesels, marinised by Vosper Thorneycroft. She cruises at 9 knots, running very comfortably at 1250 rpm. She recently returned from Cowes to Suffolk Yacht Harbour in 19 hrs - only occasionally exceeding 9 knots down the face of a wave!

the dream . . .

by Michael Spear in 1961
Founder & Chairman

Mike Spear FRICS, in 2009.

"

I had been sailing on the Orwell near Ipswich and all the other East Coast estuaries for many years, and had tried to come to terms with the problems. But when you have to trudge across a muddy beach to reach your dinghy, and then row some way out into the channel before you even reach your boat, you start to envy people who can simply walk aboard.

You read about the new marinas that are being built in the Solent and down at Brighton - all over the world in fact - and you dream a little.

The idea for the original history of Suffolk Yacht Harbour, and the information that enabled it to be written, came from the late Mrs Margaret Spear and the late Mrs Eve Jonas.

"
Until the light, or their
strength fails (usually, I am
told, at about 9 or 10pm) they
dig, dredge, bulldoze, crane
and drag their way through
tons of dark blue clay.
The objective is to build a
harbour; a 600-berth marina
with walkways and pontoons,
a club building, shop,
chandlery and car park.

THE FIELD 5 August 1971

1 one man's vision

"

It takes an enthusiast to dream. A good business brain, hard work and perspiration are vital pre-requisites for turning a dream into reality, but the motivating force must be passion - a vision of what might be.

In 1964, the north bank of the River Orwell at Levington was known only to walkers and wildfowlers. It was shallow for some distance towards mid-river and the shore side pasture was boggy and unfit for agricultural use. But a marina . . . now there's an idea.

It was the vision of Michael Spear that turned the dream of Suffolk Yacht Harbour into reality. An enthusiastic yachtsman since the early '40s, it was on a cold winter morning in 1961 that he saw the opportunity that was to bring him ten years' hard labour, countless seemingly insurmountable set backs and the most rewarding project of his life. That morning, Mr Spear, a chartered surveyor from Little Bealings in Suffolk, was carrying out a valuation for probate on the 1,000 acre estate of Mr James Stennett.

Mr Stennett's farmland, then recently inherited by his son Charles, included 60 acres of flooded marshland on the north bank of the River Orwell halfway between Ipswich and Felixstowe in a small hamlet called Stratton Hall.

The muddy saltings had been formed in 1942 when a freak tide had breached an ancient river wall constructed by Napoleonic prisoners of war. The flooding had rendered the grazing land useless. Michael Spear stood with Charles Stennett at the bottom of the farm track near the wood overlooking the flooded marshland. The question was, how could they put a value on this useless land? Could they, after all, do something with it?

Their answers formed the idea for a yacht harbour, sheltered by the wall from mud and the wash of passing commercial traffic. And that was how this story began.

The value of hindsight

It is perhaps easy now, with the value of hindsight, to see how realistic the dream indeed was.

To understand the history, however, we must put ourselves in the position of a handful of local businessmen who had a great deal of enthusiasm and limited resources. A team who were prepared to sacrifice their free time and get their hands dirty for a cause that was far from certain.

For it wasn't an amateur yacht harbour which they dreamed of, nor a 'fun' marina. Michael Spear had formed his vision whilst visiting harbours in Europe, enjoying the convenience of pontoon mooring, accessible repair facilities and a working clubhouse.

Resources which today sailing enthusiasts from all over the world enjoy at Suffolk Yacht Harbour.

The original yacht basin open
for business in 1970.

Michael Spear and his
mother Nora look across
the saltings in 1966.

2   Key Players . . .

These are the ten men who shared Mike Spear's vision and rose to the challenge of 'making it happen.' Individually, not one of them had the required experience to lead such a formidably technical project. But collectively, they amounted to an unswerveable team who, as it were, got stuck in and saw the job through.

The second part of their contribution is told in Chapter 17, page 116.

MICHAEL SPEAR

A chartered surveyor from Little Bealings near Woodbridge in Suffolk. In 1962, whilst carrying out a valuation of the 1,000 acre Stratton Hall estate for Charles Stennett he saw the potential for the flooded riverside. He is Chairman of the Board of Directors.

ERIC WRIGHT

A boat builder from Ipswich who was approached for his opinion of the project and invited to invest in it. He remained a director of Suffolk Yacht Harbour until his death in 2008 at the age of 92.

JOHN ADAMS

An architect from Ipswich who made the planning application which led to consent being granted in July 1966. He died in 2005.

CHRISTOPHER JONAS

A chartered surveyor from Otley near Ipswich, he had an engineering degree and designed most of the items to be used in the construction of the harbour. He died in 1980.

KIM HOLMAN

Naval architect of West Mersea, Essex, well known for his yacht designs. He was a member of the well-known Holman engineering family and remained a Director of Suffolk Yacht Harbour until his death in 2006.

JONATHAN DYKE

Joined as Assistant Harbour Master in September 1982, took over from Peter Phillips as Harbour Master and joined the board in Autumn 1986. He is now Managing Director.

L to R: Geoff Hubbard, Eric Wright, Chris Jonas and Michael Spear in 1970

GEOFF HUBBARD

A refrigeration engineer and company director from Woodbridge in Suffolk. He was invited to join the board of Suffolk Yacht Harbour and, in the Spring of 1970 he sailed from the harbour on a voyage to explore every marina between the East Coast of England and Majorca, logging 4,600 miles in seven months of sailing.

PETER PHILLIPS

Formerly a precision engineer in the Ipswich firm of HE Phillips and Son, he retired from business to become Suffolk Yacht Harbour's first Harbour Master in 1971 and was appointed a director of the company. He remained a director of Suffolk Yacht Harbour until his death in 1996.

NIGEL CLARKE

Joined Suffolk Yacht Harbour in 1971 as a machinery operator and soon became Chief Engineer and 'schemer', a full time position which he occupied until his retirement in 2008.

CHARLES STENNETT

A farmer from Stratton Hall, Levington, Suffolk. Charles Stennett had inherited the land including the marshland which his father had used for grazing cattle until a freak tide had broken through the sea wall in 1942. The subsequent degradation in the land rendered it unsuitable for arable farming. Charles died in 1979.

Above: A Wright & Sons 'Family Fourteen' sailing in Alresford Creek in 1975. Eric Wright's Ipswich based business produced a range of traditional family sailing dinghies during the '50s, '60s and '70s.

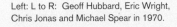

Above, L to R: Kim Holman, Charles Stennett, Eric Wright, Michael Spear and John Adams surveying the site in 1967.

Left: L to R: Geoff Hubbard, Eric Wright, Chris Jonas and Michael Spear in 1970.

3 Launching the Idea

"
The scheme for the first yacht harbour on the Felixstowe bank of the River Orwell was approved by East Suffolk Planning Committee at its meeting on Tuesday. The scheme will open up one of the most attractive stretches of the river bank below Stratton Hall near Levington.

EAST ANGLIAN DAILY TIMES
March 1967

Before Michael Spear and Charles Stennett could roll up their sleeves and start work on the project they had to draw together a team who had the necessary skills to make their vision a reality.

First, they approached Eric Wright who had an active boat building business in Ipswich. His father and grandfather had been turning out small boats since the First World War, but when his son had emigrated to New Zealand and his daughters to Canada, Wright & Sons was left without an heir. Eric Wright's enthusiasm was free to be poured into the Suffolk Yacht Harbour project. Together, these three men saw the potential for a simple non-luxury development (all kept repeating, "not a marina") where weekend sailors could walk dry-foot on to their boats at all states of the tide.

They imagined the first 12 acres housing 70 yachts, a dinghy park, a car park, a yacht club and a boatyard. They looked beyond this first stage to a 21 acre site with berthing for 600 boats by 1975.

The site was perfect, being on the Orwell, two miles up river from Harwich and within easy reach of the A45. From Stratton Hall there was immediate access to 50 miles of sailing on four attractive river estuaries. The River Orwell has one major advantage over other East Coast estuaries in that it has no shallow bar across its mouth and therefore access is unrestricted. In addition, the deep water channel at Harwich keeps the estuary open for all shipping.

The planned harbour would inhabit an open foreshore, fringed with woods just two miles downstream from the historic and picturesque Pin Mill.

In February 1967, Suffolk Yacht Harbour Limited was incorporated with an authorised capital of £60,000, made up

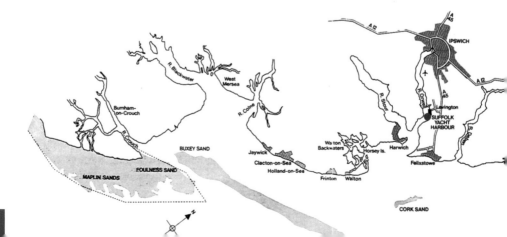

of the savings of Spear, Stennett and Wright, its three founding directors. It didn't take long for reality to tarnish the dream. As Michael Spear said some 20 years later "Frankly, I don't know how we ever did get it going . . . Building the harbour has proved a gargantuan task, but even when things looked blackest, we never felt the frustration we suffered at the hands of the bureaucrats." First in 1963 came the struggle for outline planning consent on the 12 acre site. They presented their aim as providing recreational facilities in a part of the world where they were urgently needed and converting a useless area of marshes into an attractive amenity. Not an unreasonable proposition, one might think.

Everyone involved was determined to preserve the beauty of the existing environment. They didn't want to overdevelop the site, just make it more accessible to yachtsmen and non-sailors alike.

As John Adams was to state in March 1967, "We think this scheme will enhance the beauty of the riverbank, and open it up for all sorts of people as well as yachtsmen. There are some lovely walks in the area which are not used much at present because access is too difficult."

Relaxing on a gaff cutter

The original application was followed by two further years striving for detailed planning permission. During this protracted period when disillusionment often dawned, the three original directors recruited reinforcements in the form of Chris Jonas a chartered surveyor and qualified engineer, Kim Holman a naval architect, and John Adams an architect. All had been friends of Michael Spear for more than ten years and probably needed to be, to take on such a daunting task. There was certainly more love than profit in it. They too invested their savings in the project. Each brought with him new skills, new enthusiasm and the encouragement needed to carry on. The original three by now knew that the cost of the project would be considerable and had selected the team so that fees, other than legal, were eliminated.

Later the six were joined by local businessman Geoff Hubbard as financial adviser. Hubbard too was a personal friend of Michael Spear and was introduced by him to the rest of the team. Though his involvement was largely in the boardroom, he shared the team's enthusiasm for the practicalities of the project.

In the Spring of 1970 he took his yacht, *Irene of Boston*, on a 4,600 mile round trip, visiting almost every marina between the Orwell and Majorca. It was a voyage of discovery, to enable

Launching the Idea

the team to compare the facilities they planned with the best of what was already on offer. On his return he reported, "I didn't see anything to better what we shall be offering here."

Together, over months that turned into years, they reassured the various interested authorities that Suffolk Yacht Harbour was a worthwhile development.

The Rivers Authority needed to be convinced that excavation of land behind the sea wall would cause no damage. Customs and the Board of Trade were concerned about the dangers of smuggling. The Roads and Bridges Department needed assurances that access to the planned harbour would be convenient and requested the construction of passing places along the length of road from the Levington Ship pub down to the railway crossing. Ipswich Dock Commission was concerned that any damage to the river banks might prejudice interest in the river by affecting the main channel.

The list of interested parties began to seem endless, even a local footpaths society wanted to preserve a footpath which had been impossible to walk for 20 years.

By the time all the consents were secured it was January 1967, five years after Michael Spear and Charles Stennett had first stood overlooking the site. All they had to do was find the money and the machinery and do the work!

The Land Commission Act was by this time imminent, with the appointed day for commencement of work, to avoid paying a levy' set at 1 March 1967. This short-lived Act of Parliament required that development land tax be paid on all new developments. It therefore seemed prudent to start at the earliest possible date and at minimum expense to secure a safe position.

Fortunately, the first shovel hit the mud just days before that appointed by the Act.

A sketch of the planned harbour
produced in 1967

Left: The first dragline and some rudimentary shuttering in July 1967.

Below: Levington mud in all its glory, March 1967.

" the first shovel hit the mud with just days in hand

4 Mud and Machinery

" After more than three years of preliminary negotiations, work has started on the construction of a new harbour that will provide additional berths for about 300 yachts on the River Orwell, one of Suffolk's favourite yachting centres.

FELIXSTOWE TIMES
14 April 1967

One of the most daunting practical problems was the sheer amount of mud and silt that needed moving - near enough half a million tons. This was because the harbour needed to accommodate a rise and fall of up to 18 feet of water, compared with just 18 inches in the Mediterranean.

Neap tides on the River Orwell average 10 feet, Spring tides 14 feet. In 1953 a surge of 5 feet 3 inches on top of the Spring tide caused the now historic floods which resulted in death and devastation on the East Coast. Another surge of this magnitude would leave the river waters lapping nine inches below the level of the Suffolk Yacht Harbour car park - a safe distance. At the same time the low water depth had to be a minimum of 6 feet to allow for access at all tides. These conditions would make Suffolk Yacht Harbour the nearest lock or sill-free harbour to the continent and ensure that it was popular with owners of larger craft, allowing yachts of up to 50 feet to lie afloat at all states of the tide.

Access to the marsh itself was virtually impossible, so before any equipment could be moved on to site, trial bores were taken to establish the nature of the subsoil. These showed approximately two feet of fine silt, one foot of original top soil, and 16 feet of blue and/or London clay. In order to get the dragline on to the marsh, two parallel roadways had to be constructed. Fortunately for the team, the back land subsoil was a suitable hoggin material and was dug and carted with a loading shovel.

These roadways were working walls 140 feet apart, standing at a 35 degree slope which would allow the harbour to be constructed by dragline operating between them. Contracting the

Above and below: Early aerial photos of the original two working walls in May 1967.

November 1967 - the enclosed future service area.

work out would have saved time, blisters and backache, but would have cost more than they could ever have hoped to raise. Outside contractors would have needed around £3-4 million whereas using their own labour and a tiny permanent workforce in the form of Lionel Shepherd, a tractor driver from Charles Stennett's farm, the team was able to cut the estimated cost to a quarter of a million pounds. By today's standards of construction costs, it indeed seems a minimal amount. It serves as a reminder though, that this was 1967 when a quarter of a million would have been the equivalent of at least one million in 1993. And that Suffolk Yacht Harbour Ltd was formed with just £60,000 of investment.

Even with the resources of local businessmen of the standing of Geoff Hubbard, it was an awful lot of money to raise. The financial constraints tested the team's ingenuity at every turn. A small proportion of the equipment that they needed was bought, much was made. They initially acquired a Fowler bulldozer, RB10 dragline, NCK-Rapier dragline with a 60 feet jib and Weatherhill two cu. yd. loading shovel.

With the help of Geoff Burrell, a retired pattern maker from Richard Garrett Engineering in Leiston, they built an 8 inch cutter section dredger from a sunken hull at Mistley, and a Gardner engine rescued from a lorry that had been wrecked in a motorway pile up. By literally joining the two halves the machine it cost £6,500 instead of £32,000. Chris Jonas taught himself and Lionel Shepherd, the tractor driver, to use the 60 foot jib crane and dragline which gouged out the mud and added it to the growing wall.

In January 1968, Charles Stennett got mud on his face quite literally when he capsized the barge and crane whilst digging the first harbour (p.23). Once the working walls were complete, construction could begin on the slipway and half tide scrubbing grids. It was necessary to excavate the first 300 feet of basin dry and to this end, a temporary wall was built between the two working walls. The area between was then excavated to the required depth and the banks built to the required height. Surplus material was moved by tractor and shovel along the top of the wall with the bulldozer working at the bottom of the excavation.

A reinforced slipway to the bottom of the excavation together with a reinforced scrubbing grid were   constructed

Fordson tractor and shovel clearing dragged mud from the working wall in April 1967.

The bulldozer working between the walls in February 1968.

Original steel piling construction,1967.

Mud and Machinery

In 1968, breaches to the Coffer dams caused endless delays.

Above/below: Margaret Spear (below) and Eve Carter Jonas gamely supported the earth-moving team, driving an old Commer tipper around the muddy site.

together with sheet pile retaining walls. The cross wall was then removed and excavation continued. At the same time a further working wall was being built to enclose an area for a boat park, car parking and service area.

At this stage an opportunity arose to take surplus fly-ash from Ipswich power station. This was used to construct the access road and provide fill for the service area. In two years, 150,000 cu. yds were delivered, levelled by the team's own labour and topped with 6 inches of hoggin, giving a good working base.

When, eventually, berths were ready, the pontoon walk-ways alongside were reclaimed from Harwich wartime anti-submarine defences. The uprights to which these were tethered had previously served as Ipswich trolley bus poles!

By the end of the first year's digging and dragging, one and a half acres had been cleared dry to full depth, there was deep water between two mud walls, a new sandy road and a concrete slipway. At the end of 1969, flooding set the work back by nine months. Then, as if that wasn't enough, disaster struck. Ominous-looking semi-circular cracks began to appear in the top of the wall. With a quarter of the first stage complete, the newly built wall holding back the dredged material collapsed as an undetected seam of sand took its toll. The seam had been

❝ Phase I of the yacht harbour opened early in 1970 .

L to R: Eric Wright, Mike Spear and Chris Jonas with the original piling for the scrubbing grid, 1968.

> At the end of 1969, flooding set the work back by nine months. Then disaster struck . . .

West Harbour showing the collapsed wall.

missed when the original soil test bore had been taken. If it had been discovered, the chances are that the project would never have been started. It is difficult to imagine quite the degree of disappointment felt by the seven-strong team who had toiled after work and at weekends to create Suffolk Yacht Harbour. Chris Jonas admitted in 1971 that it had looked like the end of the project. In fact, it was 'only' the end of an extra £10,000 and, toughest of all, 12 months' work. The additional £10,000 was invested in more steel piling. To be effective, this had to reach the level of the original marsh. The piles were therefore 25 feet long, tied by two inch diameter tie-rods attached to a 10 feet long anchor wall, 50 feet away.

The first 300 feet were installed by contractors and after this the team finished the work for the usual economic reasons.

Phase I of Suffolk Yacht Harbour was opened early in 1970, providing river access at low water, 40 berths, a concrete

In January 1968, the crane on the barge capsized with Charles Stennett on board.

Chris Jonas and son Tinker, August 1967.

5 First stage ends

*Seven businessmen from the Ipswich area who call themselves '**the mudlark directors**' are busy working on Britain's most ambitious 'do-it-yourself' project. During the past four years they have rolled up their sleeves at weekends and have worked as labourers dredging and digging more than a quarter of a million tons of mud and silt from the foreshore of the River Orwell.*

The most encouraging thing after all the problems was that the 40 berths ready in 1970 were all instantly booked. The setbacks and sore backs felt by the team had at least been worthwhile - people actually wanted to use their harbour facility.

The first boat to enter Suffolk Yacht Harbour in 1970 was *Merry Heart* owned by Mr Chambers of Bucklesham Garage, near Ipswich. It was followed by *Maleni* owned by Michael and Margaret Spear, *Zeelust* owned by Chris and Eve Jonas, and boats owned by Dr Burgess, R. Underwood, M. Pawsey, G. Burns and K. Duke.

At this stage, the piling was extended eastwards which required more dredging but at last this was contracted out, the contractors moving 100,000 cubic yards of mud and river silt at 19p a yard.

This work enabled Phase II to reach completion in 1971 and included the pontooning of the original walkway which was now lined with wooden slatted walkways resting on huge floating pontoons. Also, the team set out the dinghy park, car park and a corrugated iron workshop. Mains water, telephone and electricity were to follow after.

Rewards for the years of hard labour were now visible and the work itself became less demoralising and more rewarding

'Tinker' and Johnny Jonas and Lesley Spear 'helping out' in 1967

as each little step had visible results. Families were now involved too, with the Spear and Jonas children playing nearby and wives, led by Hilda Wright, providing much needed refreshments from what became known as 'Hilda's Tea Hut'.

By 1972 Phase III was complete with 170 berths, a more permanent workshop and a chandlery. The chandlery, a traditional brick-built building of around 2,000 sq ft was positioned on reclaimed land and was therefore built on a heavily reinforced concrete raft. It incorporated offices, toilets and shower facilities.

The last of the dredging for Phase III in 1972.

The 1972/3 season saw yet more steel piling to the east followed by more contract dredging during the next season. This time, a different company was employed to do the work. To cut a long and unhappy story short, the team's experience

The first stage of the project complete in 1971

with this company was both unpleasant and unsatisfactory.

They began work in December 1973 but never got to grips with the task, both plant and equipment proving unsuitable. By the spring, only two-thirds of the job had been completed in twice the estimated time and for twice the cost that had been quoted for the whole job! They eventually left the site in April 1974. This meant that the pontooning was still unfinished in time for the 1974 season but thankfully, 300 Phase IV berths were finished in time to open in 1975.

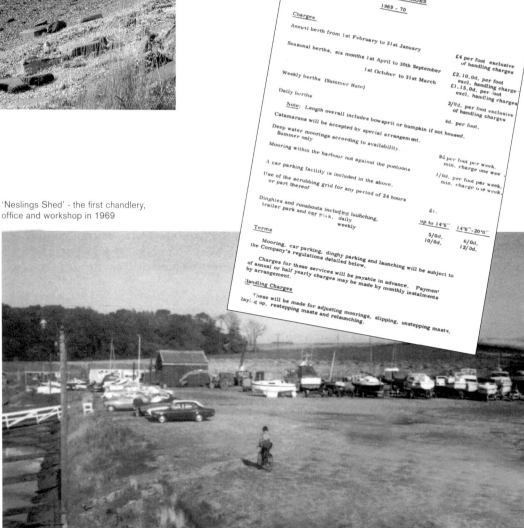

A berthing charge sheet from 1969/70

'Neslings Shed' - the first chandlery, office and workshop in 1969

SUFFOLK YACHT HARBOUR LTD.
SCALE OF CHARGES
1969 - 70

Charges

Annual berth from 1st February to 31st January — £4 per foot exclusive of handling charges

Seasonal berths, six months 1st April to 30th September — £2.10.0d. per foot excl. handling charge

1st October to 31st March — £1.15.0d. per foot excl. handling charges

Weekly berths (Summer Rate) — 2/0d. per foot exclusive of handling charges

Daily berths — 4d. per foot.

Note: Length overall includes bowsprit or bumpkin if not housed.

Catamarans will be accepted by special arrangement.

Deep water moorings according to availability. Summer only — 9d per foot per week. min. charge one wee

Mooring within the harbour not against the pontoons — 1/0d. per foot per week. min. charge one week.

A car parking facility is included in the above.

Use of the scrubbing grid for any period of 24 hours or part thereof — £1.

Dinghies and runabouts including launching. trailer park and car park.	up to 14'6"	14'6"-20'0"
daily	5/0d.	6/0d.
weekly	10/0d.	12/0d.

Terms

Mooring, car parking, dinghy parking and launching will be subject to the Company's regulations detailed below.

Charges for these services will be payable in advance. Payment of annual or half yearly charges may be made by monthly instalments by arrangement.

Handling Charges

These will be made for adjusting moorings, slipping, unstepping masts, laying up, restepping masts and relaunching.

Muddy Boots

" Suffolk Yacht Harbour's very own dredger 'Muddy Boots' has been part of the winter landscape at Levington for over 30 years

O ne of the great, unsung heroines of Suffolk Yacht Harbour is probably quite unknown to summer-only visitors and berth holders.

She only comes out in the winter. A less welcome feature of the yacht harbour is its propensity to silt up. It's a by-product of being located on the outside of a bend in the River Orwell; the tide scours away at the inside of the bend, collecting mud and depositing it back through the entrance where it gently settles on the bottom. To maintain the necessary low tide depths for our berth holders, we have to spend five months every winter from November to March sucking it up and returning it whence it came. We can only remove about a quarter of the silt each winter so it actually takes four winters completely to dredge the harbour.

Mike Spear acquired *Muddy Boots* from British Rail at Stanstead Abbotts on the River Lee, back in early 1975. She was shipped down to Levington by road in pieces and assembled on site.

Muddy Boots is a 10 inch, cut-and-suck vessel with a massive 2 metre diameter centrifugal pump.

Above: 'Muddy Boots' still going strong in February 2005, after 30 years' hard work.

Right: 1975 and 'Muddy Boots' takes to the water for the first time. The newly built workshop is clearly visible.

In an unusual 'topping out' ceremony the clubhouse was completed when the light was lifted on to the tower in Spring 1978.

6 The Lightship

"

Youth is generally full of energy and enterprise and certainly the now two year old Haven Ports Yacht Club based at the Suffolk Yacht Harbour on the River Orwell at Levington possesses both these qualities.

The clubhouse is the ex-Trinity Light Vessel LV 87, which has since been converted and has a bar and club room for dances and parties. The club burgee has a light-vessel depicted as its emblem.

EAST ANGLIAN DAILY TIMES
March 13 1976

There was one thing obviously missing from the fine new facilities at Suffolk Yacht Harbour - a clubhouse. Somewhere for visiting yachtsmen to stop and exchange stories. A place where the team could meet to discuss the job in hand and rest their legs, somewhere in which they could celebrate the near miraculous achievements so far.

Once again, the team's imagination and ingenuity were to provide them with a clubhouse of real character at a cost that they could afford. In 1975 they bought a redundant lightship from Trinity House for around £4,500. The vessel, built by Hughes in Glasgow in 1932 was originally the Mid Barrow LV87 and later completed her career as the Cromer Light Vessel. Though the lightship's interior accommodation was perfect, outside something was missing - a light. Acquiring one was a story in itself.

During the winter of 1977, Michael Spear was having a new boat built at a yard in Wroxham. Whilst passing Norwich to view the work in progress, he noticed another former Trinity Lightvessel that was complete with light and then being used as the Sea Cadet training vessel, 'TS Lord Nelson'.

Thinking that training manoeuvres required as clear a deck as possible, he suggested doing the cadets 'a favour' and removing their light free of charge. This idea was popular with the Commanding Officers, not least because the more enthusiastic boys had been climbing on to the light to peer into the bedroom windows of the hotel facing the mooring.

Suffolk Yacht Harbour's iconic Lightship has provided a welcome haven to members and visiting yachtsmen for over 35 years. It is the headquarters of the Haven Ports Yacht Club.

The cadets' lightship was moved down river by the Spears' truck pulling it from the towpath to a yard where the light was removed in another Spear 'deal'. This time, the work was done in exchange for the valuable scrap metal. The light was then put on to a low loader on its side (in order to preserve low bridges) and brought to Ipswich by road.

The lightship gave a home to the newly formed Haven Ports Yacht Club and provided room for a bar, sundeck, meeting room and committee room. The first committee was made up of Michael Spear, Eric Wright, Chris Carter Jonas and Dick Mallinson. By 1976, club membership had reached an impressive 250 and they were organising dinghy, Squib, Mirror and yacht racing.

Phase V, which followed, saw the establishment of a permanent steel frame boat store and workshop for working on boats during the winter. Together the new buildings covered 90 x 50 ft and replaced a motley collection of temporary structures.

Thus, the on-shore facilities were completed by 1975 together with berthing for 300 yachts.

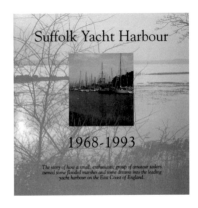

Suffolk Yacht Harbour

1968-1993

The story of how a small, enthusiastic group of amateur sailors turned some flooded marshes and some dreams into the leading yacht harbour on the East Coast of England.

In 1975, representatives of Trinity House came from Harwich in their launch and presented the directors of Suffolk Yacht Harbour with a coat of arms and a brass bell for Light Vessel 87. L to R, Eve Jonas, John Adams, Peter Phillips, Eric Wright, (receiving plaque), Michael Spear, Geoff Hubbard, five representatives of Trinity House, Hilda Wright.

This is the end of Belinda Moore's text from the first HISTORY OF SUFFOLK YACHT HARBOUR, published in 1993.

The publishers are grateful for permission to incorporate it in this 2011 edition.

7 Consolidation

1976 - 1993.

Extending the main harbour, attracting partner business to the site, increasing the range and scope of onsite buildings and constructing the lifting dock for our 60 tonne Travel Lift.

The principal activities during this period of the development were the ongoing extension of the main harbour in an easterly direction. This was largely undertaken using the Yacht Harbour's own dredger *Muddy Boots* (page 27), depositing the spoil material on the original silt pans to the west of the harbour.

A period was set aside each winter to dredge an area large enough to create several new berths. This had to be fitted into the schedule when no maintenance dredging was underway. Once a sufficiently large area had been created, additional finger berths were assembled and let.

The period also saw an expansion of the shore-side facilities and the arrival of some of the first 'partner' businesses including Clarke and Carter Interyacht, who took occupation of a new building in 1978 with R & J Marine Electronics in 1982. Part of this

Above: The Yacht Harbour in the 1980s with the first stage of offices adjacent to, and above the chandlery.

Right: Earth movement causing piling failures have been an ongoing problem - and one that is challenging and expensive.

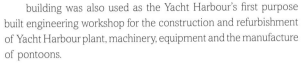

building was also used as the Yacht Harbour's first purpose built engineering workshop for the construction and refurbishment of Yacht Harbour plant, machinery, equipment and the manufacture of pontoons.

Buildings were constructed specifically to provide facilities for the following partner businesses: Bob Spalding in 1988, Parker and Kay Sailmakers in 1989, French Marine Motors in 1989 and Eastern Electronics in 1993.

The old lean-to arrangement that stored redundant equipment was pulled down and replaced with a purpose-designed paint application centre. A proper woodworking machine workshop adjoining the repair workshop was also added. Additional areas of hardstanding were created around the boundary areas of the site with previously utilised areas which were levelled and surfaced to a higher standard.

An extension to the chandlery was undertaken on the northern elevation and a year or two later additional first floor offices were also created. The old porta-cabin toilet and shower facilities were replaced with purpose designed facilities which greatly improved the situation for berth holders and visiting yachtsmen.

The Harbour escaped escaped the 1987 hurricane remarkably lightly as very few boats had already been laid up on the hardstanding. However, the two 'long jetties' K and J took the full broadside of the wind, causing some pontooning to buckle and bend which crushed three or four vessels. By the end of the following day, all the pontooning had been removed as had any damaged vessels which had been laid up on hardstanding. Pontoon repairs, refurbishment and replacements were undertaken within the following month. Probably a testament to the fact that SYH is a Harbour - it has a wall which prevented the water surging and further stressing the pontoon structure.

Above: The Great Gale of 1987 did little damage to yachts in the marina as the 'harbour wall' provided great protection from the 100+ mph southerly blast.

Below: The southern self-launch slipway opposite the harbour entrance was opened for use in 1999.

At this time several areas of original piled structure failed due to poor ground conditions and limited budget during the original construction period. The problem areas consisted of a 200 m strip in front of the chandlery and offices, 100 m section adjacent to the Lightship and an area of back wall failure of tie bars and whalings in an area between the main repair workshop and the crane bay.

During this period we constructed the lifting dock for the 60 tonne Wise boat hoist which we acquired second hand from Moody's Marina at Swanwick. It is the original 60 tonne hoist built by Wise in 1978 and we are still maintaining and running it today.

We also constructed the southern, self-launch slipway adjacent to the harbour entrance.

8   **SYH in 1993**

"

Visiting Suffolk Yacht Harbour in 1993, it would have been hard to imagine the muddy battles that the team had fought in the '60s and '70s

There were nearly 500 berths filled with yachting and motor craft of all descriptions.

The sight that greeted one in 1993 after leaving the long, well-maintained entry road was of practical, stylish design. A *chic* style that one had - by then - expected to find in the Mediterranean, not on the East Coast of England. In this respect, Suffolk Yacht Harbour had begun to fulfil those early dreams of Michael Spear and the founding directors. The facilities on offer, compared to 1975, were very impressive.

As planned, the marina had comprehensive maintenance and repair facilities. There was a reinforced concrete slipway, two boat hoists (10 and 20 tonnes), two boat cranes (5 and 20 tonnes), fuel, gas, equipment for pressure washing, resprays, epoxy coating and sandblasting. On-site workshops could offer good quality shipwright and joinery services and room for winter storage with hardstanding.

The harbour had also become home to several local marine-related businesses ranging from sailmakers to yacht brokers, marine electronics experts and engineers and suppliers of motorboats and outboard motors.

Suffolk Yacht Harbour had everything needed to provide a comfortable welcome to yachtsmen however far they had travelled. There was an extensive chandlery as well as a general provisions shop and off licence, clean well-serviced shower and toilet blocks, public telephone and ample car parking

Of course, there was also the Haven Ports Yacht Club, flourishing in the ex Trinity House Light Vessel and one of the most

A riot of colour

eyecatching and iconic clubhouses afloat. It seemed appropriate to have the centre for relaxation and refreshment housed aboard a craft that signified safety for sailors over centuries.

Hot and cold meals were served during the summer months and at weekends throughout the year. The bar and lounge on the upper deck and restaurant and lounge on the lower deck could cater for parties of up to 120 people.

In 1993 Suffolk Yacht Harbour provided a resting place for more than 2,500 visitors. Its location was proving to be one of its best selling points. Belgian, Dutch, French and Scandinavian visitors return season after season, using Suffolk Yacht Harbour as a base from which to explore the waterways of the east coast. For UK sailors, the harbour was perfectly positioned for access to the continent, with Calais just 70 miles away, Ostend 80 miles and Hoek van Holland 115 miles. All visitors had the security of knowing that Harwich harbour could be approached at any state of wind or tide.

The management remained committed to the original concept: A marina run by yachtsmen <u>for</u> yachtsmen. The team did not hold a party to celebrate Suffolk Yacht Harbour's completion, simply because they did not see it as finished.

Further developments would take place within existing planning consents, but the original determination to achieve excellence would ensure that Suffolk Yacht Harbour would be enjoyed by many generations to come.

9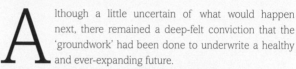

Further developments would take place only within existing planning consents, but the original determination to achieve excellence will ensure that facilities will get better still - and that Suffolk Yacht Harbour will be enjoyed by generations to come.

A lthough a little uncertain of what would happen next, there remained a deep-felt conviction that the 'groundwork' had been done to underwrite a healthy and ever-expanding future.

By 1998, the marina had expanded its maintenance and repair facilities while more marina-related businesses had arrived and set up shop on the site, to further enlarge the marina's resources and appeal to yachtsmen and motor boat owners. These included: Clarke & Carter Interyacht (1978), R&J Marine Electronics (1983), Orwell Stores (The Chandlery) originally from a container (1985). Eastern Electronics (1987), Parker & Kay Sailmakers (1989), French Marine Motors (1989) and Bob Spalding Ltd (1987).

The full story of the growth of onsite businesses (partners) is detailed in Chapter 17.

What was needed - and produced as a formal planning application in 1998 - was a MASTERPLAN for the next 15 years:

National designations

The Orwell estuary, along with the north bank of the Stour, was designated an Area of Outstanding Natural Beauty (AONB) under the Wildlife and Countryside Act 1981. This designation was extensive and covered both river banks, including the villages of Levington and Nacton.

A new planning application

Although the impetus for this application arose from a dire need for additional boat storage and car parking, it was felt that, in preparing the masterplan and statement regarding anticipated change within the next 10-15 years, it would be unrealistic to discount a major increase in boat numbers.

So a need to provide storage for an additional 250 boats, with car parking, therefore evolved and was requested by the yacht harbour. At the time, however, the western end of the marina had a great many uses, not all of them complementary to the Area of Outstanding Natural Beauty status of the area.

Boat storage on dry land was a major feature and it was felt that an opportunity existed to create a more ordered environment,

The Orwell estuary and north bank of the Stour is designated an Area of Outstanding Natural Beauty (AONB).

The Masterplan

The extensive southerly views across the marina, downriver to Felixstowe and Shotley, have been carefully preserved throughout the development programme.

consistent with the rest of the marina downstream. This was the focus for proposing an enlargement of the existing secondary yacht basin westwards, to be known as the new West Harbour.

It was considered that this would unify the appearance of the whole marina, enforce the re-piling of the western yacht basin (which would greatly improve its appearance) and remove the need for extensive boat storage on dry land at the western end of the site.

A larger yacht basin in this western location would increase the density of boats within the marina but would entail no extension of the 'development envelope'. It would extend the ordered atmosphere of the eastern end of the marina and would produce much tidier storage for the boat cradles that occupied the area during the summer months. In addition, the 'amenity' area which formed the western boundary of the site would be re-planned. New planting would be carried out, ditches cleared, a new pond scrape formed and measures taken to ensure that the silt pans, now significant for wading and wintering birds, would be adequately screened from intrusion from the marina.

Replacement 'amenity' would be offered within the field to the north of the marina, which offers excellent views over the river and a more attractive footpath route through the site (p.38). Parked cars and winter-stored boats would be removed from the marina frontage as far as possible, while acknowledging the fact that physically moving boats is a cumbersome operation that requires significant space. Suffolk Yacht

Harbour had acquired the field between the existing marina and Stratton Hall Wood in 1997, with a view to using it for boat storage and additional car parking. However, the eastern end of the field and part of the approach road had commanding views over the field, mudflats and river Orwell towards Pin Mill, and extreme care was necessary to avoid losing the vista. Consideration was also given to views into the site from the west and from the coastal paths on both sides of the river and from the river itself.

With these views in mind, an earth moving concept was evolved to screen the storage area as far as possible from both the access road and the coastal paths, while seeking to accommodate a sufficient number of boats to relieve the visual intrusion of boat storage on the waterfront. This would provide a larger area for viewing the river to maximum advantage and would also provide some screening of boats stored at the western end of the area. Planting within the field and around the northern edge would help to channel and focus attention on the river views and to conceal the stored boats to the south.

These earthworks would form the first phase of these proposals, to be followed by the piling and excavation of the proposed extension to the western yacht harbour. The dredged material was to be placed in the silt pans in a layer approximately 1 m deep. This would encompass all the excavated material, so that there would be no need for disposal offsite, and it would have the benefit of bringing the silt pans up to an appropriate level for grazing, once they had been allowed to re-vegetate naturally.

Careful consideration was given to the visual impact of boats stored ashore during the winter months. This is the section under Stratton Cliff behind the Lightship.

The Masterplan

New planting

The first phase of development consisted of extensive planting within the existing 'amenity' area that formed the western boundary of the site. The existing planting had been only partly successful, with almost total losses of some species. Careful assessment was required to ensure that only appropriate species were planted, i.e. locally indigenous native varieties that were capable of withstanding the rigours of the strong salt-laden air naturally prevalent on the site.

Consideration was also given to the fact that some parts of the field had up to a metre of unconsolidated material as a planting medium. Further factors were the proximity to the existing woodland of Stratton Hall Wood and the proposed character of planting within the field. It was suggested that it should be kept mainly open, with scrub species along the edge abutting the storage area and groups of trees at the eastern end against the access road.

Creating the harbour entrance meant re-routing the seawall footpath inland through the woodland under Stratton Cliff. The path has excellent views southwards across the marina and River Orwell. (opposite top)

Operational use

All planting was to be carried out as soon as practical. Planting in the north field would take place after the excavation of the boat storage area and completion of the surrounding earthworks.

The car park area along the marina frontage was thought likely to form part of the original Phase II development.

These proposals related principally to the need for winter storage of boats on dry land, for the reasons explained earlier.

New planting in the western
boundary 'amenity area' in 2002.

The Masterplan

This would very significantly relieve pressure for boat storage on the marina frontage, especially at the western end of the site.

During the winter months boats were to be stored in the area below Stratton Cliff, in the central space around the harbour master's office and adjacent to the western end of the western yacht harbour.

During the summer months the majority of boats would be berthed in the marina, and the storage area in the north field would be available for car parking, thereby relieving pressure on the hardstanding areas of the marina frontage.

All boat cradles were to be located in the eastern end of the storage area, while dinghies would occupy part of the western end. The remainder of the area would be available for car parking. In addition, the pipes and floats associated with winter dredging could be stored here - away from their previous prominent position.

It was also proposed that a one metre high timber retaining wall would be erected around the perimeter of the storage area, to provide a 'crisp' edge. This would be screened from the access road and the amenity area by the proposed landform and the vegetation around the storage area.

Pressure on boat storage on the marina frontage was greatly relieved by fully utilising the central area below Stratton Cliff.

Habitat Improvement

Discussions took place with English Nature and Suffolk Wildlife Trust about the possibility of improving existing seabird habitats in and around the marina - in order to:

• create vehicular barriers to protect breeding and nesting birds

• erect signs indicating dedicated new areas for fishing and picnics

• provide information on breeding birds and the need for dog control

• recharge the seaward side of the sea wall with stone and shingle to provide a more appropriate habitat for breeding oystercatchers and ringed plovers.

Oystercatcher

Foreshore Recharge Areas

Local evidence suggested that this programme was having some success in re-creating mud flats along the foreshore to east and west of the main marina. It was therefore proposed that these two areas should be extended in order to aid the re-creation of an additional mudflat. Additional wattle barricades were needed to help retain silt, and these would occupy the line of the original sea wall, subject to agreement with English Nature and Ministry of Agriculture, Fisheries and Food.

Ringed Plover

Creation of Grazing and Saltmarsh

As a result of several research projects and work undertaken by Harwich Harbour Authority and Ipswich Port Authority on the effects of dredging on the sub-tidal estuary, it appeared likely that, within the following five years, proposals will be put forward to recharge the area upstream of the deep-dredged areas, in order to prevent further erosion of the mudflats.

Under this proposal Suffolk Yacht Harbour would be encouraged to place their annual dredged material directly into the river beyond their sea wall. This would obviate the need for silt pans and would release them for alternative use, such as grazing of silt pans 2 and 3. These were at slightly different levels but distribution of dredged material over the following four years could remedy this situation.

In the short term, the outer sea wall should be shored up by the deposition of stiff clay which would help to reduce the erosive effect of wave action. It was noticed that the public footpath, which lies seaward of the outer sea wall, was only just passable.

Planting and Pond

All planting close to the river, especially re-planting at the western end of the site, between the yacht harbour and the silt

The Masterplan

pans, should consist of native tree and shrub species, selected for their robustness and ability to withstand salt spray and an exposed position.

A pond would be excavated in the existing amenity area to provide additional brackish water habitat. Planting in the north field would consist of shrub, tree and scrub species, selected to complement and extend the species in Stratton Hall Wood .

They would be planted within an area sown with an appropriate grass and wildflower seed mix to ensure ease of management. Most of the area was to be managed to create a mosaic of long grass, rabbit grazed turf and scrub. The majority of the field could be grazed, if the informal footpath were to be clearly marked and excluded from the grazed area.

Native tree and shrub species appropriate to a marine environment would be planted within the area adjacent to the harbour master's office. They would be planted above ground level in planters made of stout timbers with some excavation of the hardcore sub-base, to ensure adequate space for root growth.

These proposals were intended to address the main operational aspects of Suffolk Yacht Harbour for the following 10-15 years. It was obviously difficult to make predictions about the future, but Suffolk Yacht Harbour had a current urgent need for boat storage and a waiting list for marina berths. It was anticipated

Classic Bermudan rigged wooden yachts relaxing after another successful Classic Regatta in 2009.

Local evidence suggests that deposition of dredged material is having some success in re-creating mud flats along the foreshore to east and west of the main marina.

Huge topsail working boat making her way upriver.

that development would proceed accordingly, with detailed planning applications submitted at the appropriate times, in **three phases:**

Phase 1 : 1998 - 2000
1. Excavation of boat storage area - 24,000 cu m
2. Planting of north field
3. Planting and re-planting of amenity area
4. Erection of new signage
5. Shingle recharge of main sea wall frontages
6. Office construction for EAST and Spaldings
7. Flooding of silt pans and excavation of scrapes

Phase 2 : 2000 - 2008
1. Re-organisation of hardstanding areas
2. Entrance improvements
3. Possible deposition of dredged silt direct to river

Phase 3 : 2008 onwards
1. Excavation and piling of extension to west harbour
2. Installation of pontoons
3. Construction of new toilet block
4. Construction of further new buildings
5. Completion of grazing areas in former salt pans.

In the event - as we shall see - progress exceeded predictions by a considerable margin with the new West Harbour extension opening in early 2005 - three years ahead of schedule!

10 New West Harbour

"

The extension to the West Harbour was to be the crowning achievement of a civil engineering project that had run for over 40 years.

It looked as if it might cost precious hardstanding space, but a solution was developed.

The redevelopment of the West Harbour started in earnest in the summer of 2002. As well as providing 50 new big-boat berths, the ambitious new scheme would bring the whole marina up to the high standards of the now, well established eastern harbour. The downside of this much needed expansion originally appeared to be the loss of hardstanding space. And after studying the 'sardine can' appearance in the 2001 aerial photo, there did not appear to be an obvious solution.

But one was eventually found. It was realised that there were many examples of smaller boats arranged with lots of space between them. This was because the original Travel Lift was 20 ft wide and could not physically put boats any closer together. With the acquisition of a very clever Dutch Roodberg boat mover that could adjust its width to place boats in a row with absolute minimum waste of space, the problem was solved.

Neither did it mean losing the room to work on topsides, as a minimum separation was maintained between boats. And the overall layout of the hardstanding areas was far more efficient.

While the Travel Lift's 20 ft track width gave good spacing for big boats - it wasted space in the placement of smaller craft (right). A new boat shifter (below) was fully adjustable and could put smaller boats closer together to maximise the reduced hardstanding after completion of the West Harbour.

The re-planted amenity area to the west of the western boundary.

Classic Regatta regular 'Lady of Hamford' beating down river past the yacht harbour entrance.

Suffolk Yacht Harbour in February 2002 when the maximum number of craft were wintering ashore. Although it looks pretty well chock-a-block, a more organised approach with variable spacing freed up plenty of space to carry out the West Harbour enlargement programme.

Aerial photograph: Airviews

New West Harbour

"

By the autumn of 2002 the programme to enlarge the West Harbour was well underway with a 200 metre run of deep piling showing clearly where the new water would extend to.

The new, larger West Harbour would be able to accommodate yachts and motor boats of up to 60 ft loa. Having cleared the hardstanding area between the western boundary and the existing marina, a 200 metre run of 13 metre deep piles was sunk down the centre of the existing hardstanding area. This would eventually be the western boundary of the new extended harbour.

These piles were tied laterally underground by a series of 17 metre long, 50 mm diam steel rods to a secondary row of 4 metre piles to the west. These were sunk approximately 4 metres below the surface to provide total resistance to the main harbour edge piling once the excavation had taken place. Although the complete project took approximately two years, there was minimum disturbance to berth holders throughout the build programme which was completed well ahead of schedule.

The 13 metre piles were carried in a 'gate' holding a row of 16 which were driven in groups. Crane suspended, low noise, vibrating pile-drivers were used to minimise sound pollution.

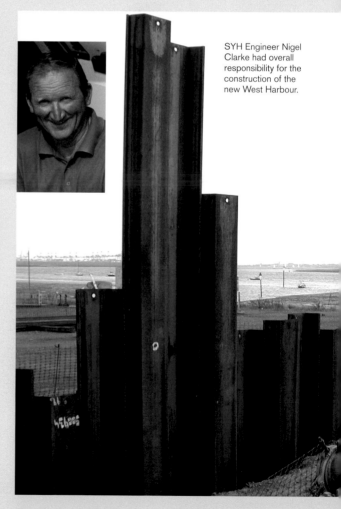

SYH Engineer Nigel Clarke had overall responsibility for the construction of the new West Harbour.

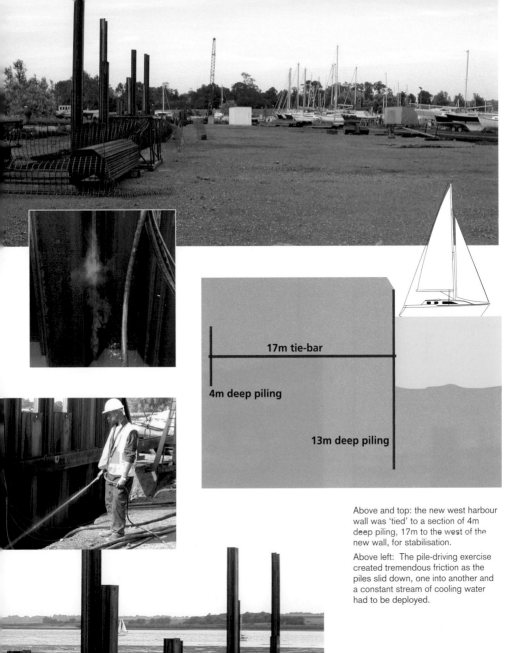

17m tie-bar

4m deep piling

13m deep piling

Above and top: the new west harbour wall was 'tied' to a section of 4m deep piling, 17m to the west of the new wall, for stabilisation.

Above left: The pile-driving exercise created tremendous friction as the piles slid down, one into another and a constant stream of cooling water had to be deployed.

New West Harbour

"
A little over a year after work began on the ambitious project, excavators made the final cut to flood the first part of the new deep water West Harbour. There was still a long way to go, but the workforce stayed on track to open early in 2005.

". . . operating in unstable wet clay, the excavator drivers had to be very accurate with their machines as the initial surge could easily have caused a mudslide . . ."

The morning of Tuesday 29 July 2003 marked a major milestone in the construction of the new, big boat, deep water yacht harbour. With thousands of tons of material already excavated to a depth of 26 feet from the new site - bordered by new steel piling - diggers set to work on breaking through from the old west harbour.

Operating in unstable wet clay, the excavator drivers had to be very accurate with their machines as the initial surge could easily have caused a mudslide which would have carried them away with it.

In the event, there was a very impressive roar as the breach was made and the excavators and their drivers kept their heads above water. Two months on and the shape of the new harbour could be clearly seen as the massive task of 'munching' away at the vast remaining area continued relentlessly.

The excavated material was used to re-establish traditional riverside grazing pastures adjacent to the site.

Below left: the new void slowly begins to fill.

Below: SYH engineers built all the new pontoons onsite.

Bottom: The new West Harbour's full size is revealed.

New West Harbour

" At last the formidable programme of excavation, piling and groundworks was completed - six months ahead of schedule. It was an impressive sheet of water.

The new West Harbour construction was completed in the Spring of 2005 and the area of water looked enormous. Yachts turning to port once inside the harbour were in for a surprise!

Of course there was much still to be done until final completion over the summer and winter of 2005 with pontoons, electrical installations and a complete new shower and laundry block to be added. Now that the hardstanding area was clear, level and re-surfaced, things were at last back to full capacity ashore - quite an achievement considering the sheer scale of the new harbour. SYH had also been conscientiously 'green' in turning the spoil from the dig back into meadow, with new tree planting.

While trawling through their photographic archives, they came across a few black and white pictures from 1972 which clearly show just how much progress had been made (see p.25).

Above: Visiting yachtsmen who had not been to SYH for a few months had a surpise in store after they had passed through the entrance in the Spring of 2005.

Left: New West Harbour filling up with boats early on in the 2005 season.

Below: The Squib fleets from HPYC and EAST with more space to spread out in the West Harbour.

Left: Superb Mike Page aerial photo of Suffolk Yacht Harbour with the newly completed West Harbour. The reorganised hardstanding along the western boundary (bottom of picture) and in the north field (left of picture) clearly illustrates the overall tidiness of the site. Compare with the 2002 picture, p.45.

11 Classics racing at Levington

"

The weekend of 15-16 June 2002 brought sunshine, fresh breezes and a magnificent line-up of 24, wooden bermudan-rigged, 1920-1970-built yachts to Suffolk Yacht Harbour's inaugural **Classic Regatta**.

It quickly developed into one of the country's best loved, best attended events for these graceful, spectacular craft.

The inspiration for this new, classic yacht regatta at Suffolk Yacht Harbour came to Jonathan Dyke during a cruise to the Isle of Wight to watch the Americas Cup Jubilee in 2001. As well as his own very beautiful 40 ft Mystery class *Cereste*, he noticed many other East Coast based classic wooden yachts among the spectator fleet. Why not an East Coast event specially for them, he conjectured?

After a very positive response to the idea from some of the key players, a total of 30 invitations were sent out - producing 24 enthusiastic acceptances. And all the 'marketing' of the event had been achieved on the telephone. Jonathan decided to be very clear about eligibility for the event: Yachts had to be of wooden construction - clinker, carvel or strip plank and built between 1920 and 1970. Bermudan was the only allowable rig. Not that there was anything against gaffers - just that they already had a multitude of events on offer on the East Coast. And this rule ensured achieving the right levels of desired *grace and pace*.

For the inaugural classic regatta in June 2002, 24 participants arrived at the startline for each of two, three-hour races down the Orwell and round a number of marks in Dovercourt Bay.

The racing was competitive and spectacular in a fleet ranging from the 45-foot vintage 8-metre *If* down to the little 27-foot Tumlare *Imari*. The two Mystery class 39-footers of John & Ira Munns, *Mystery of Meon* and Jonathan & Scilla Dyke, *Cereste*, had a battle royal at the front of the fleet - eventually being split by the breathtakingly beautiful West Solent One Design *Arrow* which finished runner-up to *Mystery of Meon*. All in all, competitors and spectators alike gave a huge thumbs-up to what was to quickly became an important annual event on the East Coast.

Left: Action at one of the starts with the West Solents getting away first.

Below Left: Pre-war beauties basking in the sunshine after Suffolk Yacht Harbour's inaugural Classic Regatta in June, 2002.

Below: The bermudan rig, pre 1970, wooden construction criteria caught the imagination and a very interesting collection of yachts came to the early startlines.

Classics

"

The second running of the Classic Regatta in 2003 saw the entry list jump to 40.

When the classic bermudan fleet reconvened at Levington 12 months later, it had nearly doubled in size. Word had spread throughout the south-east and no less than 40 thoroughbred yachts came to the startline for the second running. The formula had clearly captured the imagination of owners - and yachts arrived in Suffolk from as far away as the Solent.

The weekend of 14-15 June consisted of, like so many weekends of the remarkable summer of 2003, wall to wall sunshine and excellent sea-breezes. Perfect conditions again.

The oldest entry was *Lora* a beautifully restored, Payne Clark designed sloop with a pretty canoe stern. She was flying a new suit of Quantum Sails with a very impressive wooden rig which had been 'breathed on' by Rig Magic. Not the fastest yacht on the water but one of many stirring sights over the weekend.

Fastest machines were the lovely West Solent One Designs with Peter Brook's W18 *Black Adder* winning the Regatta after a great scrap with the W1 *Arrow.*

Above: 'Lora's' crew discuss tactics.
Right: Classic yachts stream away from their committee boat startline, led by 'Rising Hope'.
Bottom: Jonathan Thompson's pretty Tumlare 'Imari' from Aldeburgh.

" wall-to-wall sunshine and excellent sea breezes

Top: 'Lora' revelling in the summer breeze.

Above: Fastest machines were the lovely West Solent One Designs with Peter Brook's W18 'Black Adder' winning the regatta after a great scrap with the bright red W1 'Arrow.'

Left: Jonathan Dyke's 'Cereste' in hot pursuit.

Classics

"

The Kim Holman designed Stella - which nicely met the entry requirements of timber construction, bermudan rig and a build date between 1920 and 1970 - got the message and began arriving in numbers in 2004 from all the Stella East Coast hotspots.

The bermudan brigade returned in force in 2004 with over 40 yachts for SYH's third Classic Regatta.

For the first time the East Coast Stella fleet turned up in numbers and showed how well they perform on handicap. Mick Willetts' No 99 *Polaris* took the Clarke & Carter Classic Yacht Trophy as overall winner of the regatta and sowed a seed that ensured the regatta would always enjoy a healthy Stella fleet.

By 2006 - in another summer graced with relentless sunshine, the weekend of June 10/11 was one of the best for sailing - with a spanking breeze to get the best out of the 49 classic bermudan yachts that came together for Suffolk Yacht Harbour's 5th Regatta. The eclectic fleet included a plethora of ravishing yachts to delight the eye and featured a wide range of designs including Stellas and West Solent One-Designs.

The two magnificent 8-metres *If* and *Safir* burnt up the course to finish 6th and 7th overall and the three West Solents also did well, finishing 8th 9th and 10th. But overall honours went to Roland Smith and Roger Dann's very attractive Lion sloop *Leonie*.

Above: 49 classic yachts spread out across the Orwell in the early summer sun.

Right: Competition is always fierce - particularly on the startlines.

Above: Simon Cowlin & Tim Cooper's Alan Buchanan sloop, 'Rising Hope' upwind of Roland Smith and Roger Dann's attractive Lion sloop, 'Leonie' - the eventual overall winner.

Top and Left: Stellas on time at the start and (left) putting on the style in the river.

❝ Stellas starting to show their form . . .

Classics

" Another 'classic' classic regatta in 2007 was won - for the first time - by a classic 'metre' boat.

Entries reached the 60 mark !

Right: Overall handicap winner of the 2007 Regatta was the classic 6-metre 'Cailin' sailed by Sean Cullinan.

Below: The award-winning Harbour Room was brought into use for the first time at the 2007 Classic Regatta.

The entries were split into Class 1 and Class 2 handicap fleets. There was a third one-design class for the 11 Stella class yachts which have become a welcome feature of this regatta. All three classes sailed the same course.

After a very wet Friday, Saturday was a glorious sunny day with light to variable winds. Starting off the breakwater at Harwich harbour, the fleet had two races on the Saturday with the gentle conditions favouring the Stellas, West Solents and metre class yachts.

The Sunday race was again sailed in light airs with overcast, moderate visibility. However, the wind did freshen slightly during the day to allow the fleet to complete the course against a strong flood tide inside the Cork Sand.

Over the past six years, the regatta has grown in numbers and brings together a mixed group of yachts with designs from Kim Holman, Sparkman and Stephens, Alan Buchanan, Norman Dallimore, Phillip Rhodes, H G May, Robert Clarke, Illingworth and Primrose, amongst others - as well as several Metre Class yachts.

The brand new Harbour Room alongside the Lightship really came into its own this year - providing a great party venue on the Saturday evening and an excellent setting for the race officer's briefing and the final Sunday afternoon prizegiving.

Above: 2nd overall was Will Taylor-Jones sailing Richard Matthews' very quick Stella, 'Scorpio.'

Left: Sean Cullinan collects the overall 1st Place trophy at the SYH Classic Regatta 2007 from Scilla Dyke.

Classics

" By the 7th and 8th running of the regatta in 2008 and 2009, the fleet was again 60-strong and with 17 boats, the Stellas had returned to '60s strength.

For yet another year, the remarkable Classic Regatta, staged at Suffolk Yacht Harbour, increased its numbers over the previous year. For the first time the event attracted over 60 wooden, classic yachts. Once again, the Kim Holman designed, 26 ft Stellas were out in strength with eleven of these ever-popular cruiser-racers on the startline. Whatever the weather, these little, Kim Holman classics revelled in the conditions, proving as competitive in Saturday's fresh breeze as they were slippery in the light conditions on the Sunday. Congratulations to Tom Taylor Jones and *Estrella* for taking 1st overall.

The highly competitive West Solent One Designs were again, well represented while the 45 ft cutter *Croix des Gardes* certainly caught the eye. The Saturday night partying in the stylish new Harbour Room was a great success.

In 2009, the SYH Classic Regatta - the eighth - had the biggest entry and arguably the best sailing weather in the event's history. With over 60 entries - including 17 Stellas celebrating their 50th Jubilee season - the long weekend of June 12,13,14 will remain in the memory of East Coast classic sailors for many years to come.

"The weather was fantastic, absolutely superb," said SYH managing director Jonathan Dyke, the founder and organiser of the popular, annual event, which has grown steadily, year on year.

On the Saturday there were moderate breezes and sunshine, with a short race in the morning and a slightly longer one in the afternoon, in perfect sailing conditions. The Stella, celebrating its 50th season, was designed by the late Kim Holman, one of the founding directors of Suffolk Yacht Harbour.

Fittingly, a Stella again emerged as overall winner of the regatta. This time it was *Scorpio* sailed by Richard Matthews,

Peter Wilson's breathtakingly beautiful 8-metre 'If' sailed powerfully into third place in Class 1.

founder of Oyster Marine, who has an outstanding racing record in yachts large and small, old and new. *Scorpio* got clean away from the fleet in Sunday's light airs and very hot weather which provided testing conditions and a lot of stopping, starting and bunching around marks. It was interesting to note that all the entries were East Coast boats, and based between the Rivers Crouch and Alde.

After the Regatta about a dozen of the yachts headed off to the Solent for the British Classic Yacht Club regatta which took place in Cowes during July, 2009.

Top: The 17-strong fleet of Stellas cheat the tide along the Dovercourt shore.

Left: Simon Cowlin's successful Buchanan sloop 'Rising Hope' was 3rd in class 2.

Left: Classic Regatta regular, the 100 year old 'Lora' re-appeared in 2010 to show off her new gaff rig - a conversion from bermudan that had utilised the skills of the SYH yard and many of the partners.

Classics

"

After staging nine years of memorable Classic Regattas, Suffolk Yacht Harbour has emerged as <u>the</u> centre of excellence for classic yacht racing on the East Coast.

Below: Happiness is a West Solent OD.

Above: The 2010 Classic Regatta committee boat team of (left to right) Angela Pugh, Dot Marsden and Eileen Chatting.

What started in 2001 as an esoteric idea by the yacht harbour's managing director, Jonathan Dyke, had now developed into a unique annual gathering of classic racing 'aficionados'.

But with the majority of 'classics' being gaff, gunter, cutter, ketch, yawl, etc, it looked at the outset that Jonathan may well have made qualification too exclusive.

But he knew his classic yachts and what made them so special: it was the *grace* and *pace* of this elite branch of sailing that lifted it clear of the myriad events for old gaffers, barges, smacks, bawleys, quay punts etc, that he suspected would prove irresistible. And the relentless growth in entries has confirmed that his instinct was sound.*

But it is not only the classic yacht *racing* that has been a success. The SYH workshops, sail loft, rig shop, stainless fabricators, electronics suppliers etc have, collectively, become a true centre of excellence for everything to do with classic yachts - and classic motor boats.

Above: A bevy of classic beauties (and a plastic 'wide boy') head back into the marina after the Saturday racing in 2009.

Left: Coming alongside a cluster of yachts rafted up by the Lightship.

*A slight relaxation of this rule was put in place in 2010 following regatta regular 'Lora's' conversion from bermudan sloop to gaff cutter rig. The organisers will now admit pre-1970 Gaff or Gunter rigged wooden yachts, providing they were originally designed as yachts and not as working boats.

12 Craftsmanship

"

Suffolk Yacht Harbour's joiners and shipwrights are always in demand for classic yacht and motorboat repair and restoration projects.

Right: 'Dafne' looking as pretty as a picture, enjoying a summer breeze on the Orwell.

Suffolk Yacht Harbour has always had a fine reputation for its knowledge and skill when dealing with beautiful classics, whether they be timber or grp construction. Here are a few of the exacting projects the workshops have undertaken in the last few years.

'DAFNE'

A beautiful 10-metre class yacht designed by Albert Anderson and built in Sweden in 1907. This gaff-rigged beauty measures 47ft 6ins (14.48 m) loa, 9ft 8ins beam (3.0 m) with a draft of 6ft 2ins (1.88 m) and a fore and aft sail area of 970 sq ft (90 sq m). *Dafne* has a displacement of 9 tons.

She was built of Honduras mahogany planking on steamed oak and Swedish iron frames with a lead ballast keel. She still has her original mahogany panelled interior. Spars comprise a new hollow Sitka spruce mast and gaff made by 'Collars' of Oxford. All her metal work is either chromed bronze or stainless steel and there are teak shelled blocks, swept teak deck, mahogany toerails, cockpit, coach roof and king plank. Below decks, our best shipwrights and joiners made matching, new mahogany cabinet doors with intricate fielded panels. With her 30ft+ boom and shallow draft, the 47ft 6ins *Dafne* is reputedly quite a handful.

'MORNING SONG'

A much more modern yacht, and this time an S&S 34 'sister ship' to Edward Heath's famous *Morning Cloud*, built in the early '70s.

Morning Song was rescued from a premature death in the west country by London architect, Mark Foley and brought back to Suffolk Yacht Harbour who Mark felt would give her refit the proper skills and attention to detail which would befit such a graceful old lady. And living locally, he was able to keep his discerning eye on the work as it progressed.

Owner Mark Foley, who had spent much of his sailing life in Dragons, now keeps 'Morning Song' at Suffolk Yacht Harbour from where he cruises with his wife Lisa and son Emile - with the occasional low profile racing on the East Coast.

The yacht received full epoxy treatment below the waterline, a complete topside respray in Britannia blue and superstructure respray in two subtle shades of white. All the teak trim, washboards and varnished brightwork inside and out were revitalised. Every fitting, winch, hatch, window etc was removed and either reconditioned or replaced. In many cases, the original fitting was re-chromium plated. While doing everything possible to retain the originality of the yacht, SYH were able to introduce modern deck systems for easier handling without compromising her 'classic' good looks. *Morning Song's* rig was resprayed white and she was fitted with a new boom and rigid kicker system courtesy of Rig Magic who also replaced the mainsheet system and much of the rigging and cordage.

Craftsmanship

"

The early 2006 season saw an unprecedented level of work - both timber and GRP - flowing into the SYH workshops. The new workshop manager, Nick Fairhurst, was thrown in at the deep end.

Nick Fairhurst joined the Yacht Harbour as workshop manager in December 2005 following John Nunn's retirement in the autumn.

Nick had worked around boats all his life, having started a long and interesting career back in 1967. After an apprenticeship with Toughs of Teddington, he started his own boatyard on the West coast of Scotland in 1975.

He worked on a variety of boats prior to moving to Charleston, USA, to work with a maritime museum and the American Sail Training Association.

FIVE TOP PROJECTS

By February 2006 the workshops were at maximum capacity with no less than five yachts being worked on simultaneously. The new manager, Nick Fairhurst, was enjoying the challenge - particularly as three of the yachts were built of wood, his favourite material. Nick brought a new style of 'grass roots' management to the yard with an efficient new office from where he could supervise the team more effectively and enjoy much more up to date, direct communications with the directors.

He is committed to maintain and enhance the yard's reputation as a 'Centre of Excellence' for boatbuilding and repair in the east of England.

An all new spray centre opened in mid April, 2006. Previously, the paint shop was simply a sealed off area of the main workshop. The new facility enabled paint to be heated with the extraction of fumes - and was capable of lifting the temperature through 30°. Paint could be baked on and cured quickly so the turnaround time for boats got faster - even in mid season.

'Kanga'

Owner Jenny Schram. Built Bryan King in 1983 to his own design. Mahogany carvel sloop. Repairs to deck, coach roof, cabin sides, new hatches and deck gear, repairs to cockpit, re-spline topsides. Full repaint and varnish.

'Moustique'

Alan & Nicky Major's beautiful 1974 S&S Swan 41 *Moustique* by Nautor, Sweden. Topside respray, Majestic Blue, Awlgrip paint system. Her mast, boom and spinnaker poles were also repainted in Awlgrip Cloud White. *Moustique* has been extensively campaigned in east coast racing circles as well as receiving many accolades at Swan European regattas, Cork Week and other events. She is also a much loved family cruising boat.

'Andraste'

Owner Peter Arstall. Designed Bjarne Aas. Built at Fredrikstad Norway, 1964. 40 foot, long keel mahogany sloop. Repairs to coachroof, cabin trunking, bulwarks, refurbish timber hatches, spline topsides, new teak deck, toerails, stanchions, guardrails, headlinings, rewired, new galley plumbing, full paint and varnish. Steering system overhaul.

'Phaedrus'

'Kanga'

'Andraste'

'Saetta'

Above: The SYH workshop at full pelt with three wooden 'classics' and two high class grp yachts undergoing major repair or improvement work.

Moustique

Kanga

'Phaedrus'

Owner Rowan Francis. Vancouver 32 built by Northshore Yachts. Prepared for owner and his family to compete in the ARC race. Full overhaul of all services. Removal and re-bedding of toerails, windows, hatches, deck and hull fittings, updating navigation equipment. Preparation and application of Copper Coat Antifouling.

'Saetta'

Owner Peter Manning. Moody 41 designed by Bill Dixon, GRP sloop built Marine Projects at Plymouth. Major refit including new teak decks, stanchions, toerails, guard rails, rewire, re-plumb, new hatches and deck gear, reconditioned engine, new galley, upholstery and head linings.

Craftsmanship

"

The Last Ranger

Suffolk Yacht Harbour called on all its skills in the refit of this classic Nicholson Ranger 36.

'SINDUR IV'

As a first boat, this powerful, 'official' looking motor yacht was perhaps an unusual choice, with 450 hp on tap and a displacement approaching 9 tonnes. But when the owners, David and Christine Allen saw *Sindur IV* on the Hamble, it was love at first sight and exactly the sort of 'go-anywhere - in style' classic motor yacht they wanted. A deal was struck and *Sindur IV* began her second life.

NORTHSHORE & CAMPERS

The Ranger 36 marque, known for its excellent sea-keeping qualities, had actually ceased production in 1977, but Northshore moulded a final one ten years later for a client who would settle for nothing less. Uniquely, this boat had been fitted out by Camper

A stream of silky power is unleashed from the twin 225hp Ford Lehman turbo-diesels.

& Nicholson, so the joinery was to their very high standard and needed little work. The boat was sound, but very much in need of the kind of custom refit that was firing David's imagination. After long discussions with Jonathan Dyke, a no-compromise plan was agreed to return her to sparkling, 'as-new' condition.

The truth is that 12 months later - she was finished to a higher standard than when first commissioned in 1988.

A GREAT TEAM PROJECT

East Anglian Sea School boss, Peter Smith, skippered her back 'home' from the Hamble and over the next year, most of the

Yacht Harbour's on-site businesses contributed to her meticulous refit. The yard brought life back into the hull with an epoxy system below the waterline and Awlgrip spray paint application to the topsides and superstructure.

The windows were re-glazed and the wheelhouse head-linings replaced. The decks were re-caulked, doweled and sanded and a new bow thruster and anchor windlass installed. A completely new, state-of-the art, navionics package with a custom radar mast carrying a comprehensive range of instruments was added. Mr Stainless was also very active, fitting solid guardrails, bathing platform, fender and liferaft holders and other stainless trim. Quantum stitched and fitted midnight blue canvas covers to the wheelhouse and aft deck, while Rig Magic contributed a portfolio of midnight blue dock and travelling warps with colour coded whipping.

'SHE LOOKED AN ABSOLUTE PICTURE'

Down below she was not short-changed either. The soft furnishings in the saloon and wheelhouse were re-upholstered in navy leather and all the electrics replaced by John Gill. The teak and holly cabin soles were restored to their original glory and the galley refitted with new appliances and plumbing systems including a holding tank and the provision of an Eberspacher central heating system.

The helmsman's steering console was rebuilt by R&J to include modern navigation and engine management controls and a full width display of new instruments was installed over the wheelhouse screen - together with more powerful wiper motors and arms.

Finally, the twin 225hp Ford Lehman turbo-diesels were taken apart and put back together with great care - although they had only run for 1,000 hours since new in 1988!

The collective skills of the many trades and services at Suffolk Yacht Harbour will see *Sindur IV* through the next twenty years.

The wheelhouse was extensively re-modelled and re-equipped: New full-width instrument display above the screen with shaped 'blisters' to conceal three new wiper motors. The main display console was rebuilt and fitted out with chart plotter and a full set of new engine instruments.

Craftsmanship

" Suffolk Yacht Harbour's mastery of traditional refurbishment techniques were under examination with this major renovation of a 50-year-old fishing boat - and a 1960s Illingworth classic.

'SEA MARGE' & 'CHAMOIS'

This old, 35 ft double-ended, motor fishing boat was built by Smith & Hutton in Dundee about 50 years ago and converted to a private vessel some years later. In 2004, her owner, Mr P Harvey, instructed SYH to carry out major structural work and repairs to her very pretty - but badly rotted - rear end. It was quite a challenge for the shipwrights to say the least.

GROWN OAK FRAMES

Originally built from Douglas fir on grown oak frames, the port topside from amidships to the stern post was in a poor state and the workshop had to replace a number of frames and replank the hull in new larch.

The beam shelf was replaced as well as deck beams and a large part of the after deck and original sub-deck. All the old fastenings were removed and replaced with 4 in galvanised boat nails. The seams were recaulked with Egyptian cotton and Sikaflex.

Many of 'Sea Marge's' rotten frames had to be replaced with new oak while new larch planking took the place of the old Douglas fir.

Right: Five years later, 'Sea Marge' was back in the workshops for new paint and varnish - but otherwise looking in great shape

'CHAMOIS'

This excellent example of a John Illingworth designed, long keel, 'Maica' class 37-foot bermudan sloop belongs to Mr Graham Peck who usually keeps her berthed elsewhere on the east coast.

Her hull, unusually, for a boat of this period, is constructed of cold moulded mahogany on oak frames. The yard replaced large areas of the main cockpit bulkhead and also carried out repairs to the seating, teak decking and cockpit coaming.

The deck superstructure, cabin sides, toerails and bulwark cappings all received seven coats of traditional varnish from Mick McCarthy who also refurbished and varnished the instrument console and transom capping rail.

Chamois displaces 5.3 tonnes.

'Chamois' looking gorgeous in her new paint and varnish.

Mick McCarthy putting finishing touches to the masking job, prior to a topside respray.

Mick is a key player in Suffolk Yacht Harbour's team of skilled shipwrights and craftsmen who have collectively given the yard its strong reputation for quality and integrity. Mick is East Coast through and through - and proud of it.

Craftsmanship

"

Some examples of Suffolk Yacht Harbour's craftsmanship in wooden and GRP yachts.

Above: 'Croix des Gardes' in the yard showing off some of her problems, about to begin a long restoration in the SYH workshop.

Above right: Thrashing to windward in her heyday during the 1950s.

Above: 'Columbine' - looking as pretty as a picture at 30 years old.

'CROIX DES GARDES'

An elegant 50 ft bermudan cutter with a 38 ft waterline and a beam of 11ft 9ins. She has 40 mm teak planking with decks and deck structures on an oak backbone and frames, which ensure she is a powerful cruising boat. She displaces 20.4 tonnes and draws 7ft 9ins - and with a sail area of 1,129 sq ft, she doesn't hang about.

She was designed by the French naval architect Henri Dervin and built by the Bonnin yard in Arcachon in 1947 with timber hidden from the Germans during the Second World War. She then spent a period of her life in France and Italy where she was rather battered by the Mediterranean sun. Later in life, she was trucked to northern

. . . thrashing to windward in her heyday . . .

France, before being sailed back to Ipswich and moved to a barn near Cambridge for the winter of 2007/08. She was relaunched in June 2008 in time for the Classic Regatta at Suffolk Yacht Harbour but her full restoration may well continue for some years yet.

The first part of this work has been completed: we removed her keel, refitted new wrought iron keel bolts, carried out repairs to her rudder, including fitting a new rudder gland, assisting the owner with replacement chain-plates and re-galvanizing strap floors.

Work was also started on renewing her topside planking.

PLASTIC CLASSICS, TOO

While our workshops and shipwrights have earned a repu-tation for their skill with the restoration of classic wooden boats, we're not lagging behind with the quality of our work on grp yachts and motor cruisers.

Columbine - a Leisure 29 - is a good example. Designed by Frank Pryor and built by Cobramould, the class was launched in time

Left: Contessa 26 hull lines bear more than a passing resemblance to the Folkboat.

Below: 'Kelita' is a very fine example which has regularly sailed in all weathers.

for the 1980 London Boat Show. The 29 was a stretched Leisure 27 with the extra two feet being added to the cockpit length.

This example has had a full antifoul, Awlgrip respray and a number of other cosmetic improvements for a new season and looks as pretty a she did in 1980.

'KELITA' - CONTESSA 26

The Contessa 26 is one of the most enduring models in British yacht design and Kelita is a very fine example which has regularly sailed in all weathers.

Now that she's had a spell in the yard, she is in many ways, in better shape than when she was new 40 years ago - and she's certainly ready for another 40 years of thrilling sailing.

Her bottom was osmosis treated and re-epoxied and her Ferrari-red topsides have been treated to a deep, Awlgrip repaint. All her mahogany brightwork including toerails, cockpit and main hatch have been reconditioned and revarnished. New pumps and hatches were fitted, as well as nav lights and a new array of halogen quartz cabin and chart table lights.

Rig Magic and Mr Stainless also had a part in the restoration with a new boom and mounting brackets.

'SERENA' - OYSTER 45

Serena is a fine example of the ever popular Oyster 45 Deck Saloon - this version being bermudan sloop rigged. She was built circa 2000 and was, predictably, in virtually 'as new' condition and entered the yard for a pre-season topside refurbishment and polish, new stainless cleats and the installation of transom davits to eliminate the tiresome chore of dinghy deflation and inflation.

Serena was also the 'guinea pig' to receive the first example of our new, teak-clad toerail, by workshop manager, Nick Fairhurst.

Above: As well as the comprehensive schedule of work carried out on 'Serena', our ingenious workshop manager created a technique for cladding standard aluminium toerails with teak, to create the appearance of a solid toerail. The capping pieces are sawn to shape, scarf jointed and the finished result has the real look of a bulwark about it.

Left: 'Serena' and 'Dafne' in close company in the workshop.

13   People Power

"

A Great Team

Any organisation is only ever as good as the people it employs. Year after year, Suffolk Yacht Harbour has been blessed with a rich core of inspiring and talented employees who share a pride in their work with a fierce loyalty to the company.

In the first chapters of this book we recorded the extraordinary achievements of the original pioneers at Levington who, virtually with their bare hands, ground out the first holes in the mud that would eventually join together and form a recognizable yacht harbour.

By the new millennium, the yard was on a steep learning curve developing skills in response to the arrival of more advanced technologies within the boatbuilding industry. New, high-tech materials were refining structural procedures, providing greater strength in conjunction with lighter weight.

Paints had become 'coatings' with much greater performance and life expectancy, and the practice of curing paint in ovens was becoming the norm rather than an expensive option. Spray painting boats was developing as the standard practice with boatowners' increasing preference for high gloss finishes.

All this new technology meant our boatyard teams needed to confront the acquisition of new skills and procedures. The yard has been very fortunate in their willingness to absorb new methods and re-train as necessary.

As the harbour itself has grown in size, the boat movement teams have also learned new skills and the operation of more sophisticated machinery. Computers have made their mark - not only in the management of stock in the chandlery but also in the running of the main office and accounting system as well as in the management of ever more complex projects in the boatyard. Visiting boats were soon demanding - and receiving - wireless internet connections to carry on work or stay in contact with their offices. Security has become an absolute priority with millions of pounds worth of boats in the marina. Advanced CCT systems have been installed to monitor the movement of boats into and out of the harbour. Vehicles too, are strictly controlled in and out of the site. All this progress has relied very heavily on a reactive and flexible workforce, and in this we have been especially fortunate. Here are the stories of some of these excellent people that make it all happen:

BOB GIBBON
Boat movement manager

CHRIS WYARRT
Travel hoist operator

CHRIS NUNN
Berthing manager

Bob arrived at SYH in 1995 for a summer job in the chandlery following four years at uni, graduating with a degree in engineering product design.

To cut a long story short - the product design job never appeared and Bob signed on permanently at the yacht harbour at the end of '95. He moved from the chandlery into the complex logistics of boat moving with Chris Nunn and more recently was involved in the re-arrangement of all the hard-standing spaces during construction of the west harbour. Bob cannot afford to make mistakes in his job - but he does admit to one: he brought the lovely motor cruiser 'Juliagee' ashore one Friday evening when she was due to be committee boat at a regatta next morning! As soon as he realised, the troops were rallied and she was re launched in the nick of time.

Four years studying design have certainly left an artistic mark with Bob and he is a particularly creative amateur photographer - as can be seen by his striking winter Orwell sunset (left).

He has a passion for speed on and off the water. He has owned a pretty quick RIB and now has a Seaskate 16 Dory called 'Doris'. He also enjoys customising and competing in very powerful 4WD vehicles.

He is married to Emma and they have three children, Charlotte 6, Barnaby 4, and Martha, 7 months.

Chris has been working with boats on the East Coast all his life and before arriving at Levington in 1995, had spent the previous 23 years working for yacht transporters Debbage of Ipswich.

This involved moving all manner of craft including taking a 65 ft ketch from Kings yard in Burnham to Tilbury docks. The work at Levington was very seasonal with the big rush to get in for Easter and out by the end of September. Chris first went afloat at Pinmill at the age of 10 in an old smack's dinghy with an ancient Seagull on the transom and learned to trawl for shrimps with his mates.

Later on he owned 'dozens' of boats and became the proud owner of the smart 26 ft Seamaster 815 'Woolee Monkee' which he cruised and raced locally in the Three Clubs Series - then sponsored by the Evening Star with a big cup and prize money.

When not sailing, he found time to build a house for his daughter in a kindly donated corner of his Dad's garden in Woolverstone.

Lucky girl!

Chris Wyartt's Seamaster 815 'Woolee Monkee'.

Like so many of the staff at Suffolk Yacht Harbour, Chris has been on the team for a very long time. Since he first arrived as a teenager back in 1984, he has steadily taken more and more responsibility and now heads up the complex business of traffic control in the marina.

Chris is a family man from Ipswich with a 22-year-old daughter and two sons of 16 and 10. His family have always been involved in boating and his father has a fishing boat and a Westerly Longbow which he manages to borrow from time to time.

Berthing Masters for the 2003 season were: (left to right) Roger Devonshire, Roger Hanes and Peter Leason.

Chris actually had a boat of his own - an elderly Pioneer 9 which languished on the hardstanding at SYH for more years than anyone can remember. He eventually disposed of it and now enjoys a simpler boating life with a Captain RIB powered by a 50hp Yamaha.

The Berthing Manager is ably supported by a team of expert Berthing Masters who keep a firm grip on the daily allocation of berths to visitors throughout the season.

Left: Orwell sunset, photograph by Bob Gibbon

People Power

LOUISE LOUGEE
PA to Jonathan Dyke

MICK McCARTHY
Boat repairer

" It's the variety in her job that she loves so much, as well as the people she works with and the ever changing views from her office window.

Top: Louise and 'Minsmere' getting airborne at a CCI Three day event at Aldon, Somerset.

Louise has worked at the Yacht Harbour for over 15 years. She started out as secretary to both Jonathan Dyke and Mike Spear but her responsibilities have spread into countless other areas as the years have passed.

It's this variety in her job that she loves so much, as well as the people she works with and the ever changing views from her office window.

'No day is ever the same" she says "which is what makes the job so special.'

Boats are not really number one with Louise, although she occasionally ventures out with her husband, Clarke & Carter's Duncan Lougee in his Rustler 31. (Page 95). But after work, she cannot wait to get home to their 4.5 acre smallholding in Dedham where she breeds horses for three-day eventing.

She's also an event rider of considerable ability.

She currently has two horses - 'Sea Captain' and a very successful thoroughbred called 'Minsmere' who took her into the top 50 of 175 mostly professional riders at a three-day event. Louise covers a lot of the cost of her passion by teaching others to ride - including Duncan - who is not a bad horseman now either and hunts a big Irish bred animal called 'Max' - short for 'Maximum Comfort'.

Mick McCarthy is a key player in Suffolk Yacht Harbour's team of skilled shipwrights and craftsmen who have collectively given the yard its strong reputation for quality and integrity.

Mick is East Coast through and through - and justifiably proud of it. Born in Burnham in 1958 he joined Petticrows at the age of 19 in their famous old ramshackle buildings tucked away behind the Royal Corinthian YC. He was quick to learn and developed skills with wood and varnish, fitting out and maintaining the fleets of local Corinthian and Royal Burnham one designs.

In 1983 he moved along the seawall to Tucker Brown's yard where he got to grips with bigger yachts and bigger machinery - at the same time adding to his repertoire of boatyard duties including lifting and launching boats and laying moorings.

With the opening of Burnham Marina - and the increasing number of clients with GRP boats, Mick attended Lowestoft College to learn all about working with GRP and further add to his versatility at the Tucker Brown yard.

He came to Levington in 1990 and has continued to hone his GRP repair skills over the years.

Mick used to sail on his Uncle's Contessa 32 which he greatly enjoyed and is open to crewing opportunities. He lives in Felixstowe where he does a bit of sea-fishing and enjoys gardening.

STEVE MARTIN
Shipwright/Joiner

DES COWAN
Maintenance

NIGEL & TERRY CLARKE
Chief engineer/shipwright

Steve Martin has been working with wood since he left school and joined the reproduction antique furniture makers, Ratcliffe & Sons of Kelvedon as an apprentice.

After a year he decided to 'go back to school' and in 1970 enrolled at a government training skill centre in Letchworth to broaden his woodwork education. Not really inspired by the prospect of a life on building sites, a friend suggested boatbuilding - with its complex shapes and compound curves - as a more appropriate outlet for Steve's skills and he found interesting repair and fitting out work for two years with Norton Marine at Heybridge Basin.

In 1972 he got the break he had been looking for and joined the legendary R D Prior in Burnham as a proper trainee shipwright. Steve remembered Murray Prior's support for the young lads at Priors - and the way they were allowed to continue their studies on day release at Southend Technical College. After ten happy years in Burnham, Steve uprooted his life and moved up to Whisstocks in Woodbridge to begin another chapter.

After 18 months, he took the plunge and bought the little house in Woodbridge where he still lives today. Another ten happy years passed, building proper boats, before Whisstocks ran into trouble. He finally arrived at Suffolk Yacht Harbour in 1999. Apart from working in wood, Steve's other passions are his 24-year old BMW R80-ST flat twin motorbike about which he says: "I'm waiting for it to become a valuable classic."

Des Cowan is a very interesting man. His weather beaten complexion and wiry build implies a high level of fitness - and it came as no surprise to learn that he spends a lot of time at sea on his Contessa 33 'Eclipse', which he bought brand new at the Southampton Boat Show in 1984.

'Eclipse' has been berthed at SYH since 1985 and in spite of having a long and successful racing career - including winning the first Yachting Monthly Triangle race - she still has the gleam and shine of a much loved and cared for yacht.

Des ran his own steel & aluminium cladding business for 25 years, until he suffered a disastrous 25ft fall from scaffolding in 1998, breaking his back and putting him in hospital and out of work for 18 months. His road to recovery started by taking over the catering on the Lightship in May 1999. A year later, this led to an offer of a full time appointment with the Yacht Harbour to take over all aspects of harbour maintenance. Eleven years later, Des could not be happier in his job:

"It's the variety that makes it so fulfilling. Whether I'm fixing a roof, fitting an extractor fan or replacing a pontoon, it's always challenging work which involves mixing with lots of lovely, interesting people."

'Eclipse'

Nigel Clarke was a major part of the Suffolk Yacht Harbour scene almost from day one, in 1969, when he arrived after a period at Ipswich Plant Hire learning about big machines and civil engineering.

Since that time when there was one pontoon and 25 boats, he has headed up the whole marina engineering programme, including overseeing the very ambitious West Harbour project.

His son **Terry,** also went as an apprentice to Eversons Boatyard in Woodbridge straight from school and came to SYH in September 1994 as part of the team working mostly in GRP and composites. He left SYH in 2004.

Both men were devoted to sailing from an early age and sailed together on Nigel's Popcorn 23, Trapper 28 and more recently on the Pioneer 10 'Yasu' in which they won Aldeburgh Week in 1993 and 1995. Crew shortages changed the emphasis more to cruising, rather than racing the Pioneer while Terry concentrated on sailing his Blaze singlehander at Alton Water, following a 2-man dinghy 'career' in Cadets and Larks.

Nigel retired in 2008.

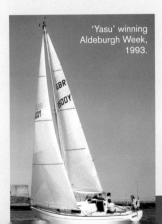

'Yasu' winning Aldeburgh Week, 1993.

People Power

JOSHUA MAJOR
Project manager/estimator

SIMON GREEN
Workshop technician

Joshua leaving Harwich Harbour in a hurry in his old half-tonner 'Smiffy'.

The first thing that strikes you about Joshua is his beaming smile and outwardly happy disposition.

This is a man who is clearly very content with his life so far.

"It's really fun to come to work" he reveals, which is not a thing you hear every day.

His passion for sailing and boats started at a very early age - clearly inherited and inspired by the antics and successes of his grandfather, Mike Spear. Joshua was a natural sailor, and quickly rose through the ranks of Optmist, Topper and Laser on the Deben, before getting his first taste for keelboats with the East Coast Squib fleet.

After leaving school, he started pouring his energies into the retail boat market, at the same time as satisfying a thirst to 'get out' more. While with Wittey Marine, Hamble he did some selling for the Italian RIB builder, Marlin - including one to Jensen Button.

By then Joshua realised he needed to refine his education and decided on a degree course at Southampton University in Watersport Studies and Management with the incentive of a 'proper job' at the yacht harbour.

He got his degree, and at 24 found himself on a steep learning curve of all the skills needed in the running of the marina.

One day he might be up the river, picking up a yacht, the next compiling estimates, sourcing boatyard materials or assisting with ongoing yacht harbour projects. It's about 60-40 between office work and 'out and about.' He's learning it all - and loving every minute. And somewhere along the line he found time to earn a commercially endorsed Yachtmaster certificate.

In yachting circles, one often meets those who dream of sailing around the world. And others who just talk about it. Now and again one even comes across an actual round-the-world project that's made it past the planning process. But it comes as a considerable surprise to meet a clean-cut chap, making a fine job of re-spraying the topsides of an old Swan 48 in the SYH workshop, who has already done a full circuit!

Simon Green is Felixstowe born and bred. After Deben High School he completed an engineering apprenticeship at Ransomes in Ipswich and qualified after four years as a general engineer. He inherited a love of boats, and sailed dinghies at Felixstowe Ferry, sharing ownership of a Fireball.

Keen to put his engineering skills to the test, Simon went to India in 1987 and worked on huge, 2000 ton 'walking dragline' machinery. The work took him all over the subcontinent - to Varanassi, Hydrabad and Calcutta, before returning to Felixstowe.

He was soon off again, first to Manchester, the Middle East and finally Ireland - building massive container cranes and 'straddle carriers.' The work was well paid and Simon finally had saved enough to look for a suitable ocean cruiser. He settled for a robust,1974 Carter 39 which he found in Majorca and sailed back to Ipswich before spending a happy year preparing her for a 'lengthy' voyage.

He is now slowly re-furbishing a 29-footer to explore the East Coast Rivers - which he knows nothing about!

RICHARD GADD
Chandlery manager

ANDREW DUNNAGE
Paint coating technician

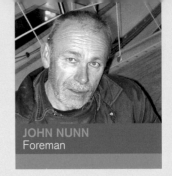

JOHN NUNN
Foreman

Richard Gadd has been a familiar face at the Yacht Harbour and took over from Jenny Mummery as manager of the Chandlery early in 2007.

After many years in charge, Jenny is taking a well earned break and reducing her hours by at least one day a week to do a lot more sailing on her beautiful yacht, 'Fanfare.' Before he arrived at Levington, Richard had spent most of the previous 12 years 'at sea' - as mate on a number of Thames sailing barges - engaged in the business of corporate hospitality. Much of this time he was sailing as mate aboard the P&O barge 'Will' (formerly 'Will Everard').

'Will' was one of the last, and largest, barges to be built - in 1925. She was all steel, weighed in at 150 tons, measured nearly 100' loa and set 5,500 sq ft of sail. Richard covered a great many sea miles on barges, taking clients to some of the far flung outposts of western Europe.

The demands of a new, young family finally brought Richard ashore in the late '90s to his home in Pinmill and very soon to his new life at the marina. He still has sailing barges in his blood and regularly helps sail 'May' to success up and down the East Coast - while keeping a Wayfarer in a mud berth at Pinmill, just for pottering. Richard has lots of plans to improve the chandlery, in particular to review the range of spares and smaller items so that customers have greater accessibility to find what they need more easily.

Andrew is one of the marine industry's new breed of 'technical' craftsmen - and enjoys the much more scientific approach to the traditional skill of painting.

He began his career in 1997 with a general boatbuilding apprenticeship in the workshops while he did three years studying at IBTC, Oulton Broad and a further two years at Lowestoft College. He qualified in 2002 with NVQ and City & Guilds skills including laminating, woodwork, painting and varnishing - where his expertise and interest have really developed. Andrew explained how advanced the new coating systems have become: "On 'Sindur IV' for instance, we adopted a multi-coat epoxy underwater system. Each layer is chemically keyed to the next so in effect you end up with a single, highly durable skin. Temperature and humidity are critical in this process. Adherence to technical specs and data sheets are key to achieving a first class result."

Andrew is Ipswich born and bred and his grandfather was a traditional yacht painter who was responsible for aiming the youngster at the marine industry. Andrew has recently bought a house in Ipswich and for the moment, confines his water-borne activities to high speed wakeboarding. Someday however, he wants to learn to sail!

Andrew applying high tech coatings.

John retired in 2005 after over 20 years at Suffolk Yacht Harbour and in that time was, for sure, one of its greatest assets. Apart from being a superb craftsman (pictured above putting the finishing touches to a fabulous new teak deck on the Swan 44 'Avista') he had the unflappable temperament which ensured the relentless smooth running of the yacht harbour workshops. He had his own boat continuously from the age of ten and built this Yachting Monthly Senior while an apprentice shipwright at Whisstocks, Woodbridge.

Other wooden boats followed including a Deben Cherub and a 'Z' 4-tonner before getting the racing bug with his Seamaster 925 in which he won the Haven Series in 1980. He also crewed for Mike Spear on 'Moustique' and spent three years campaigning the SS34 'Morning All' - sister ship to the legendary 'Morning Cloud.'

After retirement, John upped sticks and moved out to Spain where he continues to enjoy life in the sun.

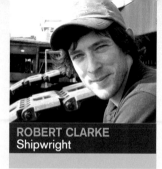

ROBERT CLARKE
Shipwright

SHELLEY ROBINSON
Chandlery assistant

People Power

" Robert trawled the internet and spotted a worn out but pretty three-quarter decked keelboat by designer Knud Reimers - much on the lines of his better known Tumlaren but with an elegant transom in place of the canoe stern.

Robert is 27, long and lean and moves deftly around the workshop with the easy manner of a man who understands boats.

He has been part of the yacht harbour landscape since he left school at 16 and started weekend work in the chandlery, quickly learning the boat business.

He is the son of a mechanical engineer and grew up surrounded with tools and machinery. His best subject at Orwell High School was

After more than a year of spare time work, the hull of Robert's boat was ready to move on to the next stage.

CDT (craft, design & technology) and by 2002 he had been taken on full time in the SYH workshop, developing his skills under the guidance of the 'master', John Nunn.

In three years he had become an accomplished shipwright working with wood and GRP while achieving his level 3 City & Guilds certification on day release at Lowestoft College. In 2007, he took a year out to ski the world - chasing the ski seasons to New Zealand and Whistler in Canada.

With that out of his system he returned to work at the yacht harbour - resolved to find an interesting wooden boat project of his own. He trawled the internet and spotted a worn out but very pretty, three quarter decked, keelboat by Danish designer Knud Reimers - very much on the lines of his better known Tumlaren but with an elegant transom rather than a canoe stern. She had been lying ashore in deepest Wales for eight years and was exactly the sort of 'project' he was looking for. She travelled back to Suffolk on a borrowed trailer. Since then, with the help of original drawings from the Swedish Naval Museum, Robert has made and installed 40 new oak frames, new floors, splined and re-fastened the fine Honduras mahogany hull and removed the keel. The ancient Vire petrol engine will be replaced with a Yanmar 1GM and then there's the rig . . . he plans to build new spars himself from sitka spruce.

Robert lives in nearby Nacton and spends most Saturdays working on the boat. At other times he loves mountain biking, water-skiing, wake boarding and crewing on Des Cowan's Contessa 33 'Eclipse'.

Shelley is the smiling face of the chandlery at Suffolk Yacht Harbour and continues to love the job she talked her way into a few years ago.

Which wasn't difficult. With many years sailing under her belt on the luxury charter yacht circuit around the Caribbean, USA and Mediterranean - not to mention nine Atlantic crossings - she ticked all the boxes!

Shelley grew up around boats, even learning to walk on the ample decks of her father's 1924 built, 46 ft Channel Yawl, 'Klang 'II'. This wonderful old yawl was originally used as an English Channel pilot boat, ferrying passengers between Plymouth and the Channel Islands.

Above: Shelley getting her sailing 'fix' at the sharp end of Rick Gillingham's successful Dragon 'Navaho'.

Dragon's Den

Nowadays, Shelley gets her sailing fixes at the sharp end of Rick Gillingham's successful Dragon 'Navaho', based at Aldeburgh Y C. This Petticrow built boat is pretty quick and results have been as high as runners-up at the Nationals.

Shelley has a son Jake, 19, who lives in Bournemouth.

"What's the nicest thing about working at Suffolk Yacht Harbour" she was asked?

"The lovely people I work with" she replied.

JENNY MUMMERY
Chandlery specialist

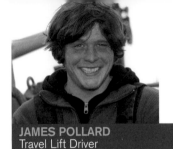

JAMES POLLARD
Travel Lift Driver

Before she worked at the yacht harbour, Jenny Mummery was a fairly regular visitor in her elderly gaff cutter 'Cachelot'. Built in Folkestone in 1897, this lovely old yacht had an illustrious history; not only was she once owned by Sir Lancelot Elphinstone, the Queen's cousin, but she was also one of the Dunkirk 'Little Ships.' On one of 'Cachalot's' visits in 1989, Derek Newman, the chandlery manager, asked Jenny if she would consider assisting him on a permanent basis. And the rest, as they say, is history.

Jenny first developed a taste for sailing while still at school in Devon - not in dinghies like most children, but starting as she meant to go on - on a gaff cutter. Sailing has been a way of life ever since. Interestingly, she does not consider sailing a 'passion' - but does revel in the freedom it gives her:

"With a boat" she says, "you can wake up in the morning and just say . . . I think I'll go."

'Cachalot' was eventually sold with a desire for more space and more performance - answered in the shape of 'Fanfare of Essex', the wonderful 48 ft ex ocean racer designed by Kim Holman and built by Berthons in 1964 which is now very much part of the SYH scene.

But with a draft of 8 ft, Jenny points out that East Coast cruising requires more than a little concentration!

Jenny has seen a huge advance in technology in the chandlery over the last few years but enjoys the challenge of staying ahead of the game in order to advise customers on making the right choice of kit for a particular job - be it a chart plotter, type of antifouling or a new halyard.

At 24, James is very amiable and enthusiastic about his job, evidenced by his beguiling smile which is virtually a permanent feature, underneath his thick mop of straw coloured hair.

He started dinghy sailing in Cadets and Larks at Waldringfield SC on the Deben but later preferring the independence of singlehanders like the Topper and Laser. He wasn't really certain about a career at this stage, but sensed an aptitude for boats and an outdoor life.

He enrolled at Swansea University for a two-year course in 'Watersports & Adventure Tourism Management' which seemed to fit the bill. As well as good management skills, he also achieved RYA Instructors' qualifications in dinghy sailing and windsurfing - 'an instant passport to summers afloat' as James described it. To prove the point he spent a happy couple of years doing just that with Rockley Point on Poole Harbour, and as beach manager at their centre in south west France.

Back in the UK he was attracted to a job advertised at SYH and three years on, has done very well as a 'protege' of Chris Wyarrt, and is now fully licensed to drive the travel lifts and the Roodberg boat shifter.

James now finds himself with more responsibility and authority which he has met with genuine enthusiasm. Like so many staff at the yacht harbour, he clearly loves his work and feels he may be able to fulfill some of his aspirations without moving too far afield.

Away from the yacht harbour he is a bass guitarist for the increasingly successful rock band 'Man from Reno'. In the last two years they have won a key music competition and signed an important recording contract with Ambiel Music.

Above: James has an 18ft lift-keeler 'Kit-Kat' which he bought from a Woodbridge boatyard and is perfect for singlehanding and teaching friends to sail. He keeps her at the yacht harbour.

Below: As well as the main 40-tonne travel lift, James is also licenced to operate our custom-built boat shifter which places boats into awkward spaces.

People Power

"

The first eighteeen staff member biographies on the previous four pages are taken from their detailed profiles printed in Harbour Light each issue since it started in 2002.

Here are another twelve key members of the team who all richly deserve a mention here.

Sara Hopkinson, Chandlery Assistant.

Ian Theobald, Building/pontoon repair and maintenance.

Rex James, Chandlery assistant.

Angus McWalter, Dredger Driver.

Eileen Tichal, Accounts, Purchase Ledger.

Tim O'Leary, Boat Repairs and coatings.

Malcolm Chambers, Engineer.

Julia Clover, Accounts, Sales Ledger.

Howard Snow, Shipwright.

James Mallett, Boat Hoist Driver.

Ben Clegg, Boatyard Trainee.

Alistair McMonagle, Berthing Master.

Steve Baggaley, Crane and Boat Hoist Driver.

Right: Harbour crane used principally for mast raising and lowering and also the only load cell weighing facility in the region.

Below right: 60 tonne boat hoist for larger vessels over 40 feet and/or in excess of 10 tonnes.

Mechanical Power

"

Our talented and loyal staff of men and women are our most valuable asset by far. But over the years we have assembled an interesting, hard working line-up of machinery which delivers a range of custom power that keeps the marina humming at peak efficiency.

Above: General purpose lift for accessing masts and carrying out building maintenance

Above right: Hoist for lifting and positioning smaller boats

Right: Mobile crane for reaching the parts other cranes can't reach

15   Harbour Light

"

The power of the press.

During 2001, an approach was made to Jonathan Dyke by marine industry marketing man, **Martin Treadway,** to consider the creation of a Suffolk Yacht Harbour, twice-yearly newspaper.

He already had a track record of successful newspaper production in the industry for clients such as Proctor Masts, Topper International, Hunter Boats, Hood Yacht Systems, and Ovington Boats. He then produced a 'visual' for what he had provisionally called **'Harbour Light'** and this immediately caught the imagination of the SYH board.

Twenty issues later, with a circulation of 8,000, the little colour newspaper continues to be the voice of the marina and keep the onsite businesses, berth-holders and visitors up to date with everything that goes on at the Yacht Harbour.

Top: John Parker, Parker & Kay Sailmakers, has been an advocate for 'Harbour Light' from the beginning and really understands the newspaper philosophy.

The very first issue of 'Harbour Light' arrived on the marina and 5,000 doormats in the early autumn of 2001. Its distinctive look, strong photography and bright and breezy editorial style struck an immediate chord with readers and partners alike.

The first front cover featured the glistening, sapele veneered topsides of *Madam*, a 70 ft custom sloop which demonstrated the advantage to boat owners of dealing with SYH - with all the facilities available on one site.

The boatyard, with skilled joiners and shipwrights, a custom paint and varnish shop, expert spar and rigging services at Rig Magic, premium sailmaking at Parker & Kay Sailmakers (now part of the Quantum Sail Design Group), R&J Electronics for the most advanced instrument and navigational equipment, French Marine Motors, inboard engine supply, installation and servicing, Bob Spalding Marine for outboards and sportsboats and - more recently - Mr Stainless for stainless steel tube and sheet fabrication.

This first issue introduced the main personalities on and around the yacht harbour and generally gave the harbour's businesses - we now call them 'Partners' - an opportunity to 'set out their stalls' in a much more personal and 'chatty' way than would have been possible in a brochure or sales leaflet.

No news is bad news - and bad for business!

Martin brought some compelling arguments to the table for the creation of 'Harbour Light', including the thought that a company newspaper keeps in touch with clients - current and prospective - in a friendly and frequent way. This encourages ongoing dialogue. A newspaper generates confidence. It is perceived as impartial. It shows <u>what others say about you</u> rather than what you say about yourself - in your (expensive!) brochures.

Above: Clarke and Carter are brokerage market leaders with long serving staff who are highly experienced in racing, cruising, bluewater sailing, charter, powerboating and boatbuilding.

Left: Nigel Theadom's young rigging company - Rig Magic - needed all the publicity it could get in its first years. Nigel did his bit by winning everything in sight in his X-332 Crikey V! - now he had the perfect place to tell everyone about it and capture the competitive East Coast rigging market.

Rig Magic is coming up for 11 years old as this book goes to press and continues to flourish.

Harbour Light

"

In the eagerly awaited second issue, the front page featured the first 'Staff Profile' - in this instance it was the yard foreman, John Nunn, who retired in 2005 after 21 years at the yard.

Each issue generates much speculation on who will be the 'guinea pig'. As the issues stack up, the number of possible victims continues to reduce.

This process lays firm foundations for future new business. New business for the Partners who were each investing in the success of 'Harbour Light'. In many cases, 'Harbour Light' has provided much of the annual marketing effort for the partners in the local area at an exceptional price.

Twice a year, Martin spends a couple of days on site, to interview each of the partners and obtain the ingredients for their next feature in the newspaper, based on what they have achieved and what their plans are for the next period. This will entail note-taking or recording, photography and the collections of references and other support material. Sometimes it can be like 'getting blood out of a stone', the editor reports, but nearly always each partner is pleased when they see the results and start to enjoy the benefits of the publicity.

By issue No 3 in the Autumn of 2002, the Harbour Light had developed a beam to 'light up' the fluttering

SYH burgee. More importantly 'Harbour Light' was able to report on the first Classic Regatta which had taken place earlier in the year to great acclaim.

This issue also set out the ambitious plans for the new West Harbour which was well underway (see West Harbour, page 44). In fact for the next few years the newspaper was, usefully, able to keep berth-holders and visitors fully aware of the build programme and the critical dates they could expect .

A bit of a breeze . . .

The weather produced the headlines for the 4th issue in the Autumn of 2003 when 110mph threatened to recreate the appalling conditions of 1987.

It had been blowing very hard all night, and with conditions deteriorating further as Britain woke up to the end of British Summer Time, we were soon to realise just how dramatically the summer was about to end.

❝ *With winds up to an estimated 80mph by 0900, all marina staff were urgently summoned to check the most vulnerable pontoons and double up warps on the most exposed craft. By this time about sixty berth holders had also turned out to lend a hand.*

Boats ashore on props and cradles were all checked and extra supports were added.. The gale reached its peak by around 1400 when a gust of 110mph was recorded at Ipswich. The strongest gust recorded at Suffolk Yacht Harbour was 87mph. The swift action of the staff and support lent by berth holders ensured that damage was restricted to minor topside scuffing, a couple of bruised and grazed pulpits and one or two broken navigation lights.

But it was all a bit too close for comfort!

Above: 'Rigging in the strangest places'. Issue No 4 carried Rig Magic's interesting account of fitting a new rig to a yacht in Grimsby.

"In the light of day we were surprised to find 'Magnum' in receptive mood alongside the back of the old Grimsby Fish Market - perfectly placed under a lofty block and tackle. With such planning and a huge crowd of helpers from the very excellent Humber Cruising Association, the job was done in no time and we were back at Suffolk Yacht Harbour by 7pm that evening."

Harbour Light
is published by:
Suffolk Yacht Harbour
Levington IPSWICH
Suffolk IP10 0LN
Telephone:
01473 659465 and
01473 659240
Fax:
01473 659632
Email:
enquiries@
suffolkyachtharbourltd.uk
Produced for
Suffolk Yacht Harbour
by Martin Treadway
mjt@easynet.co.uk
www.martintreadway.co.uk

NEWS FROM SUFFOLK YACHT HARBOUR

harbour light

www.suffolkyachtharbour.ltd.

NO 4 SPRING 2003

The friendliest, most welcoming, independent yacht marina on the East Coast

WELCOME!

from Jonathan Dyke and
Mike Spear, Directors
Harbour Light No 4 is packed
with news from Suffolk Yacht
Harbour and our fantastic
group of Partner Companies
who make this harbour so
different from any other.

Suffolk Yacht Harbour
STAFF PROFILE NO 3

The morning of Sunday
27th October 2002
showed all the signs
that we were in for a repeat
of the great gale of 1987 -
almost exactly 15 years earlier.
It had been blowing very
hard all night, and with conditions deteriorating further as
Britain woke up to the end
of British Summer Time, we
were soon to realise just how
dramatically the summer was
about to end.

110mph from the southwest

It was all hands on deck as British Summer
Time ended on Sunday 27th October with
hurricane force winds threatening to bring
havoc to the marina and the boats within.
For a while, it looked distinctly unprom...

Harbour Light

"

By the Autumn of 2004 and three years into the newspaper's history, 'Harbour Light' No 7 was reporting the dramatic impact of the new West Harbour.

Six months later, No 8 was able to report that the new extension had opened ahead of schedule in April 2005.

Above: No 8, Spring 2005, carried this aerial shot of the marina giving a very nice 'overview' of the new West Harbour which opened ahead of schedule.

"then turn left into open water . . ."

" *If you have not been to the yacht harbour for a few months - you're in for a big surprise.*

The new West Harbour is now full of water and the area we have created looks positively enormous. If you turn to port once inside the entrance, you'll see what we mean.

Of course there are many more pontoons to put in place yet and the electricity and water supplies will be installed over the winter. We are also about to start building a very smart new toilet/shower block/laundry ready for the scheduled completion date in Spring 2005.

Now that the hardstanding area is clear, level and re-surfaced, we are at last back to full capacity ashore - quite an achievement considering the sheer scale of the new harbour.

We have also been conscientiously 'green' in turning the spoil from the dig back into meadow, with new tree planting. While trawling through our photographic archives, we came across a few black and white pictures from 1972 which clearly show just how far we have come!

Below: In the Autumn of 2006, the late summer heatwave refused to cool down with the result that no-one wanted to lead the rush to bring their boat ashore.

Another dramatic cover photo told the story.

Harbour Light

"

The Autumn 2006 issue featured a dramatic new stormy sky 'masthead' at a time when the never-ending summer meant that berth-holders were reluctant to bring their boats ashore. The cover photo perfectly illustrated the task facing the berthing team.

Below: Quantum Parker & Kay announced their selection as sailmaker of choice for Nick Bubb and Pete Cummings' attempt at the Shetland Round Britain & Ireland Race in the trimaran 'Kenmore'. After a relatively trouble-free start to the race, breaking the mast off the west coast of Scotland was a mighty blow and looked like ending their chances.

A Herculean effort from sponsors and many friends got the spar repaired in primitive conditions and saw 'Kenmore' finish the race comfortably inside the time limit - and even ahead of other 30 foot trimarans on the water.

Mark Wingar (left) '**Mr Stainless**' opened a new workshop for business at Suffolk Yacht Harbour in April bringing high quality stainless steel tubing and fabrications to the marina

Pulpits, pushpits, guardrails, radar arches, boarding ladders, bathing platforms, were now available on site.

Right: This issue also contained news of Nigel Theadom's (Rig Magic) crack East Coast team retaining their X-332 National title at the class championships on the south coast - sailed under the flag of the Royal Southern YC at Hamble. 'Crikey VI' became the first X-332 ever to win this title for a second time.

Harbour Light

"

By 2008, higher postal rates levied on large envelopes had necessitated a reduction in the size of the newsletter from A3 to A4. But by doubling the number of pages, readers got more content than ever. And the smaller format quickly gained a universal 'thumbs-up'.

The new format meant that the Yacht Harbour stories could now occupy both front and back covers while still only using the same actual space as the old A3 cover. In a way, 'Harbour Light' had become more of a magazine than a newspaper.

The new format gave the newsletter a fresh lease of life and coincided with a huge increase of commissions for the boatyard, especially in the 'classic' sector where SYH's reputation for fine, accurate and sensitive restorations was developing year on year.

'All under one roof'

The impressive range of skills 'all under one roof,' as it were, had by now, established Suffolk Yacht Harbour apart from any other marina on the east coast. Almost everything an owner could possibly need for - or have done to - his boat was available onsite!

And *Harbour Light* continues to broadcast this important message to its ever increasing readership.

The first 'Meet the Professionals weekend and progress on the new building occupied the cover of issue no 19.

And ten years after the first issue, 'Harbour Light' No 20 was able to announce that Griff Rhys Jones would open the new **Harbour Centre** on Easter Saturday and that this book would be published on the same day.

In 2010, the autumn issue, No 19 (above right) announced a new 'Meet the Professionals' weekend in conjunction with the annual Clarke & Carter Yacht and Motorboat Fair in October.

As *Harbouring the Dream* goes to press in March 2011, *Harbour Light* marked 10 years in print and its 20th issue - with the announcement that the new **Harbour Centre** would be opened by Griff Rhys Jones on Easter Saturday 2011 - at the same time as the publication of this book.

16   Perfect Partners   Haven Ports Yacht Club

"

The Haven Ports Yacht Club with its distinctive headquarters in the retired Trinity House Light Vessel No 87, is a major feature of Suffolk Yacht Harbour. It has been providing first class food and drink and a warm welcome to visiting yachtsmen since it first opened in February 1974.

Bermudan rigged classics raft up alongside the Lightship during the classic regatta.

The Haven Ports Yacht Club was established early in the yacht harbour's history and its famous headquarters - Trinity House Light Vessel No 87 - have become synonymous with the warmest welcome for yachtsmen on the East Coast.

Now more than 35 years old, HPYC remains very much a 'members' club'. It provides a convivial atmosphere below decks, with function rooms and a first class professionally run bar and restaurant that is open virtually every day, throughout the year. It's a great facility for members and visiting yachtsmen - especially those who have had a bit of a 'dusting' en route.

Haven Ports Yacht Club also runs and administers local yacht racing with spring and autumn series for local and IRC classes together with the popular Boxing Day regatta.

In the '70s and '80s, HPYC staged a number of major class regattas including the Squib Nationals and the East Coast Dragon championship in the late '70s, and the Sonata Nationals in 1980. More recently, it has been the venue for the Annual Port of Felixstowe Regatta and, since 2001, it has run the increasingly

The Haven Ports Yacht Club organizes much of the yacht racing series and trophy races that take place on this part of the east coast each year.

There are Spring and Autumn series of six races for Class 1 & 2 IRC yachts, a Summer club handicap series of four races, a number of individual club handicap trophy races and a very popular Class C Frostbite, four race series in November.

popular Suffolk Yacht Harbour Classic Regatta which brings a spectacular fleet of over sixty classic wooden yachts to the River Orwell for a week's racing and socialising every year in early summer. (see pages 52-63).

Visitors enjoy deck areas on the Lightship with their magnificent views across the marina and River Orwell.

Partners   Clarke & Carter Interyacht

"

From early in the yacht harbour's history, a growing number of onsite marine businesses - the 'partners' - have enhanced the range of facilities on offer.

The first of these in 1978 was the yacht broker, Interyacht, now known as Clarke & Carter Interyacht.

Stephen Carter (right) and Duncan Lougee have helped build Clarke & Carter into one of the largest yacht brokers in the country.

Now with four offices at Suffolk Yacht Harbour, Neptune Marina, Ipswich, Burnham on Crouch and Gillingham, Clarke & Carter offer the biggest yacht and motorboat brokerage on the East Coast.

"Small enough to care, large enough to matter . . . "

Stephen Carter thinks this sums them up pretty well. Their continued success, he believes, is due to staff professionalism and an ongoing investment in technology - at the same time keeping a broad sense of humour - *and* a personal touch.

New technology

This is very much a people business and Clarke & Carter have continuously invested in new computer software to enable them to respond to all telephone and online enquiries immediately without losing the personal touch.

Enquiry rates are running at an average of 150 a day from their website, press advertising, repeat business, customers' referrals and many other sources.

Strong sales - new and used

The Clarke & Carter Yacht and Motor Boat Fair takes place every year in late October. This show is the highlight of the brokerage market on the East Coast and always produces well over 100 boats on show - more than a third of which find new owners by the end of the weekend! It is a unique opportunity for used yacht and motorboat buyers to compare many craft in the same place at the same time - without the need to drive all over the country.

Clarke & Carter have also enjoyed Main Agency status for Jeanneau Yachts for many years and the products from this manufacturer continue to please their clients. They have been particularly successful in recent years with a price advantage that clearly exists over many domestic manufacturers - even some brokerage yachts.

Trading-up policy

Naturally, C&C conduct trade-ins against new yachts that they supply and take the attitude that if they offer a client the estimated retail value for their boat as a trade-in then this will enable them to purchase a new yacht. Unlike many manufacturers and agents, they will consider almost all yachts for trade-in and do not charge a sales commission if they sell her prior to the new yacht arriving.

Clarke & Carter's Duncan Lougee spent the winter of 2009/10 refitting his Rustler 31 'Vaquero' for the 'Jester Challenge' single-handed Plymouth-Newport TransAtlantic race starting on 31 May 2010. He had completed a trouble-free 'shakedown' race to the Azores in 2008.

Duncan began the main race in 2010 which proved to be an exceptionally windy and hairy crossing. After failure of mast fittings, he reluctantly had to retire 700 miles from the USA coast, returning home via the Azores for repairs.

For many years the autumn Yacht & Motor Boat Fair held at Suffolk Yacht Harbour has brought together about 100 used yachts and motorboats for buyers to look at, all in one location at Suffolk Yacht Harbour. The Boat Show for Brokerage Boats.

Company History

Clarke & Carter was established in 1978 in West Mersea. The company ran an office at Woolverstone from 1983 until 1990 and moved the head office to Levington in 1985 when Interyacht Ltd (established in 1949) was acquired. At that time they merged the two companies to form Clarke & Carter Interyacht Ltd. The four offices are on the prime sites at the largest marinas in their areas and encompass the most popular sailing rivers of the region.

Since 1978 the company has sold in excess of 7,000 boats of all descriptions - both sail and power, ranging in price from £1,000 to £300,000. There is usually a choice of over 200 used boats on the market at any one time.

Over the years C&C have represented a large number of yacht manufacturers from which they gained much experience. These include Albin, Baltic, Bowman, Contessa, Dufour, Elan, Fisher, Freedom, Jeanneau, Moody, Parker, Sadler, Seamaster, Sigma, Southerly, Starlight, Westerly, X-Yachts and Yamaha.

Partners   R&J Marine Electronics

" Since coming to Suffolk Yacht Harbour 1982, R&J Marine has been East Anglia's favoured source of marine electronic equipment and has built a reputation by supplying, configuring and installing electronics to suit every type of vessel.

Julie Clark, managing director, has run R&J Marine Electronics with her daughter Amy since 1999. John Meade heads up the technical and installations department.

An R&J engineer goes aloft to fit new masthead wind instruments.

R&J offer friendly and informed advice and a full range of electronics for communication, navigation, entertainment, security and safety. The fact is, choosing and installing today's marine electronic systems demand specialised technical skills - and R&J Marine Electronics are your local experts for sales, service and installation of all this equipment.

Sail or power, private or commercial, large or small, there is always one piece of kit that will provide the best performance for any given task. R&J are confident they know what it is.

Installation

Fitting electronic equipment is a delicate business and there are an awful lot of things to go wrong - especially if it is necessary to pierce the skin of the boat. There are also power supply implications as well as consideration of the terms of the warranty.

Will the insurance cover remain valid even if it seems that no-one was at fault? R&J are licensed installation engineers for all the equipment they recommend and supply so there is the security of knowing that the work has been carried out by experts and is underwritten by guarantee. And none of the guarantees on the equipment itself will be compromised by the installation.

Working with R&J gives clients real peace of mind.

Guarding their reputation

R&J Marine is East Anglia's favoured source of marine electronic equipment. They've built a reputation by configuring and installing electronics to suit every type of vessel.

They offer friendly and informed advice and a full range of electronics for communication, navigation, entertainment, security and safety.

The fact is, choosing and installing today's marine electronic systems demand specialised technical skills.

In Ipswich, too.

R&J Marine Electronics Ltd opened a new branch office in the centre of Ipswich in 2002. Situated at the Ipswich Haven Marina, with 180 berths in the Wet Dock, the marina is only a few minutes walk from the town centre.

Above: R&J have a smart showroom at Suffolk Yacht Harbour where buyers can try out new equipment for themselves.

Left: R&J Marine Electronics celebrated their 25th anniversary in 2002 at the newly opened Ipswich branch on Ipswich Yacht Haven.

Below: 'Gudgeon' is a shallow draft, 42 ft Yawl, built from pitch pine and mahogany on grown oak frames in 1920. R&J Marine installed a state-of-the-art, electronics package in the old lady in 2010.

Partners   Bob Spalding Marine

"

Bob Spalding Marine was one of the earlier companies to open for business at Suffolk Yacht Harbour in 1988.

The company also boasted the best facilities in the southeast - ashore and afloat - for the sportsboat, water-skiing and boat fishing enthusiast.

Tim Reinman has been the driving force behind Bob Spalding's continued success.

The standards that this highly respected company adopted when it was founded by World Formula One Powerboat champion Bob Spalding over 35 years ago are still very much in practice today. It is this unequalled sales and service guarantee that has created their reputation and forged them into one of the largest international marine sales companies in the UK for the products they distribute.

These include outboard engines, outboard powered sports boats, waterski and wake board equipment, RIBs and tenders, sports fishing boats, specialist clothing and personal watercraft,

Along with the help of a dedicated team of highly trained factory engineers and professional staff the company has gone from strength to strength providing unrivalled advice, sales and service on the many products they represent, accommodating yachtsman, fishing boat and sportsboat owners and enthusiasts alike.

Exceptional Products

The extensive product line up includes premier brands of sportsboats, fishing boats, dories and yacht tenders, There is also a formidable line-up of inflatable tenders and RIBs from the best know brands. To complement all their boat ranges Bob Spalding Marine Ltd are an exclusive distributor for the class leading range of two and four stroke outboard engines

Service & Prices

The company continues to strike a balance between supplying quality products at competitive prices while maintaining the high level of after sales and service support expected by today's clientele.

From 1988 onwards Bob Spalding Marine occupied this large site at the western end of the marina, with workshops, showroom, offices and enough outside space to display many new and secondhand boats.

For 2010, the operation moved to this new site to the left of the main gate - formerly know for many years as 'The Pit'.

Partners   Parker & Kay Sailmakers

"

The Parker and Kay loft at Suffolk Yacht Harbour manages to combine the 'hands on' touch of a friendly local sailmaker with the solid technical background required to design sails for boats as diverse as local 'pocket' cruisers and world girdling Mega-yachts.

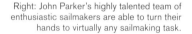

Right: John Parker's highly talented team of enthusiastic sailmakers are able to turn their hands to virtually any sailmaking task.

Below: Andrew Farthing in the busy canvaswork division producing boat covers, sprayhoods, awnings, dodgers and sailcoats.

"It's not always easy to get the balance right" says John Parker, who set up the loft with Peter Kay back in 1989. Peter runs Parker & Kay's Hamble based Design Studio and Sales Office and generates the high level of race yacht business from the ever burgeoning Solent race circuit.

Parker and Kay maintain a close relationship with leading textile and cloth manufacturers allowing the partnership to offer the latest advances in sailcloth design. These include custom made cloths utilising the very latest fibres like Kevlar, Spectra, Vectran, PBO and Carbon. There is a commitment to continuous research and development using advanced design software to produce optimised sail shapes for the maximum race winning potential - as well as cruising longevity.

Back in the 'real world' at Suffolk Yacht Harbour, John Parker's highly talented team of enthusiastic sailmakers are able to turn their hands to virtually any sailmaking task - as well as canvas products and all-weather equipment of the highest quality.

The large loft can handle big-boat projects like the sails for the recently built Spirit 100, much featured in *Harbour Light.*

Racing successes on the East Coast and Solent - as well as in the international arena - are far too numerous to record here.

John Parker is justifiably proud of Parker & Kay's racing pedigree - but emphasises that this is precisely what makes them the right choice for making your cruising sails which will perform better and last longer than those from an 'ordinary' sailmaker.

"We even reckon that our dodgers and sprayhoods are better designed and better made because of our race background" he claims, grinning.

The Suffolk loft continues to expand with a 30% larger extension to the loft floor completed in 2008. This has opened up the ground floor for clients to come and talk through their requirements in comfort, away from the hum of machines aloft.

Why not invite one of the team on board your boat for a real hands-on assessment? Parker and Kay may be one of the biggest sailmakers in Great Britain but they still want to make *your* sails.

And whatever your specific requirements may be - from international racing to East coast cruising, Parker and Kay have the specific resources to address them.

John Parker at the sharp end of a new Spirit 76 - adding his special 'touch and feel' to the headsail.

Neil Manning at work from one of the sewing pits in the loft floor.

Partners

French Marine Motors

"

The Suffolk Yacht Harbour branch of French Marine Motors was one of the first businesses to open on the site in 1989 and has developed a solid reputation for top quality engineering.

Following the sad death of long-term French Marine manager Kevin Butters in December 2006 his shoes were filled by Jason Carrie. Jason was Kevin's right hand man for many years and took on the challenge with relish.

French Marine's 2003 engineering trio of Kevin Butters (left), Jason Carrie and Matt Pearson with examples of their work load.

There's precious little about marine diesel engines that Jason Carrie (above) has not come across in the many years he's been selling them, installing them, and taking care of them. He's just the sort of bloke you hope will stick his head through the hatch when you've been struggling to breathe life into a dead engine for hours. At Levington, he is now very ably assisted by two engineers, making a formidable trio who together are almost certain to solve any mechanical problem, however tricky it may be.

The French Marine Motors group is run by Chris and Mike French from their Brightlingsea Waterside headquarters and impressive marine chandlery. As well as the Brightlingsea and Levington centres, French Marine Motors has a workshop and chandlery at Titchmarsh Marina on the Walton Backwaters and has more recently established a wholesale distribution centre for engine parts in Norwich.

New installations

With no special loyalty or limitation to any specific make of engine, Chris French explains that clients receive "totally impartial advice on the correct engine for their particular requirements."

'Nordic Eagle' with her new 3-cylinder Yanmar diesel fitted amidships by French Marine's Brian Caney. The ancient Volvo Penta MD2 sits forlornly under a sheet of plywood awaiting disposal.

Simon French (left, son of Mike French) and new apprentice Ross Copsey joined Jason at Suffolk Yacht Harbour in 2008.

French Marine Motors have been supplying marine engines for 50 years and have the experience and equipment not only to supply new engines but to fit, commission and trial installations of new engines.

French Marine are the Dealers for Yanmar, Volvo Penta, Scania, Vetus, Yamaha, Mercury, Seagull, Bukh, Sabre, Perkins, Mermaid and more. This means that French Marine can offer you the customer the best choice of new engines.

They endeavour to provide the best choice and price and add value by supplying expert advice based upon the 50 years of experience gained in the field.

Keeping it in the family

In spite of advertising for nearly eight months, Jason had not been able to find anyone suitable to back him up at Levington, so Simon French was brought over from Head Office. In spite of the long journey, he really enjoys the work at Levington and has recently taken on some interesting commercial projects.

Wind Farm support

One of the UK's largest wind farms began construction in 2007. The wind farm is located five miles off Clacton on the Gunfleet sands. When construction is complete there will be 48 wind turbines in total, helping to contribute to the government's plan to cut CO_2 emissions.

French Marine have negotiated the major contract to service the Perkins generators on a 24 hour call out basis. In anticipation of a significant role in this operation, Simon has attended the mandatory Sea Survival course.

The neat and tidy installation of a new Yanmar 2YM-15 into a pretty little Frances 26. It was a 'shoehorn' operation as the old engine was the much smaller IGM-10. As well as the powerful new engine installation, the Frances 26 was also fitted with a new and larger propellor matched to her 15 hp engine. The old Yanmar IGM-10 readily found a new owner as these popular, low cost diesels seem to go on forever.

Partners   East Anglian Sea School

"

The man or woman
who serves their sailing and
navigational apprenticeship
on the rivers and estuaries
of the east coast of England
can subsequently sail all
other waters with
reasonable confidence

HAMMOND INNES

Right: Peter Smith has shaped East Anglian
Sea School as one of the most successful
training establishments in the country.

Below: The Pico dinghy fleet and its modular
floating pontoon stowed in its marina berth.

Bottom: Dinghy sailing class ready to be
ferried out to the pontoon.

E ast Anglian Sea School was founded in 1973, starting life as a small family business on the River Blackwater called East Anglian School of Sailing. It has since grown into one of the foremost Royal Yachting Association (RYA) sea schools in the country having trained over fifteen hundred adults in 2010 alone, with an excellent reputation built on the quality of the training, facilities, craft and catering.

Thirty-eight years later it is still owned by the second generation of the same family and has been around for as long as the Royal Yachting Association training scheme itself.

The best instructors

The school moved to Suffolk Yacht Harbour in 1999 and now has 45 mature, patient and experienced instructors, qualified to the highest standards in Sailing, Motor Cruising, Motor Boating, Power Boating and Dinghy Sailing.

Training is run using a fleet of *Strata* yachts, motor cruisers, powerboats and dinghies from Jeanneau, Fairline, Ribeye, Wayfarer and Laser, all maintained to MCA standards.

A wide range of courses is available to cater for people new to boating, right through to experts in all areas from Start Yachting or Helmsman's courses, Competent Crew, Day Skipper through to Coastal Skipper and on to Yachtmaster and Yachtmaster Ocean. Courses are run all year round, on weekends as well as during the week.

Study on your own boat, too

One of the Sea School's specialties is own boat tuition, where an experienced instructor is put on to a customer's own boat (yachts, motorboats, sports boats or ribs) and will teach whatever the owner wishes.

This includes commercial boat training for all of the fishing, maritime and construction industry including wind farm support and safety boat cover.

Yacht and motor boat charter

EASS can also offer yacht and motor boat chartering of their own craft where clients can charter the school's boats, either for just one day or a whole week, allowing time to explore all around the east coast of Britain. The charter yachts are modern and equipped to the highest standards, offering exceptional levels of comfort and performance.

Following the Strata fleet's success in Fastnet races, this has now become a feature of the School's year whereby students can take part in this prestigious event, combined with the 'Around Britain' cruises in three, two-week legs.

Top: The 24 participants from the 2009 Rolex Fastnet Race.

Lower: The School's 2009 Ribeye Rigid inflatable with 250 hp Yamaha power.

Lowest: A dinghy school Wayfarer fitted with an asymmetric spinnaker system.

Above left: 'The fleet's in' - in 2008 including two new Jeanneau Sun Odyssey 36i performance cruisers like the one above.

Left: Strata 6 enjoying some brisk conditions off the Isle of Wight soon after the start of the 2007 Fastnet race.

Rig Magic

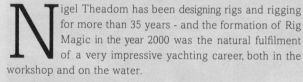

" In the eleven years since Rig Magic opened its doors at Suffolk Yacht Harbour in 2000, Nigel Theadom's innovative rigging shop has established a winning reputation with cruising and racing yachtsmen.

Below: Nigel's long line of winning yachts have born the 'Crikey' name. Here Nigel's X-332 'Crikey V!' holds her nerve on port tack, on her way to winning six out of seven races in class at Cowes Week 2003. Nigel went on to win the prestigious 'Black Group' championship at the same regatta, as well as back-to-back X-332 National Championships in 2005 and 2006.

Nigel Theadom has been designing rigs and rigging for more than 35 years - and the formation of Rig Magic in the year 2000 was the natural fulfilment of a very impressive yachting career, both in the workshop and on the water.

Twelve years running the rig division at Fox's in Ipswich while filling one of the biggest trophy cabinets on the East Coast, provided both the technical 'magic' and a deep understanding of rig performance in terms of both racing speed and cruising efficiency.

He has developed and produced rigging solutions for singlehanded round-the-world yachts, Arctic explorers, bluewater cruisers, tradewind travellers, and countless cruising and racing yachts-folk enjoying more local waters.

Rig Magic at Suffolk Yacht Harbour took off from Day One and greatly enhanced the facilities for berthholders as well as attracting clients from all over the UK.

The addition of Jonny Ratcliffe and Sam Smith to the team very soon after opening, effectively doubled capacity overnight

and freed up Nigel to seek out other projects and - importantly - negotiate agencies from prestige hardware manufacturers like Harken, Spinlock and Selden Spars.

Rig Magic knows the good and not so good aspects of just about every piece of kit on the market. And because they have no contractual allegiance to any one manufacturer, clients get really impartial advice which saves lots of wasted expense.

Rig Magic perfectly complements the other 'partners' based at Suffolk Yacht Harbour who between them offer a combined service not found anywhere else on the East Coast - possibly in the UK.

In particular, Rig Magic works very closely with John Parker and his Quantum sail loft next door to develop and produce sail handling systems not found anywhere else in the UK.

Below: Rig Magic gave this classic 'Peter Duck' ketch a major performance hike with this efficient, fore and aft rig.

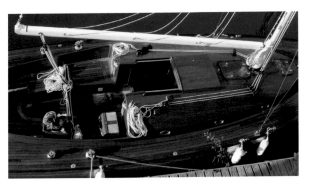

Top left: Rig Magic designed the deck layout of this very beautiful new Spirit 46 and supplied/installed the white painted carbon mast and boom.

Above left: Rig Magic were invited by Stephen Jones to develop the design of the all-carbon rig for this beautiful, one-off 49-footer undergoing trials on the Hamble.

Above: Many hands make mast work: Jonny (left) Nige and Sam make final checks before another big stick is raised.

Left: Sam at work in the custom mast shop.

Partners   East Anglian Sailing Trust

"

The East Anglian Sailing Trust's primary aim is to enable people with disabilities to enjoy the freedom and excitement of sailing in the Squib fleet on the River Orwell and further offshore in EAST members' cruising yachts.

Colin Williamson has been EAST's hard working keelboat secretary since 2003.

The Squib keelboat racing fleet and safety RIB on their pontoons in the West Harbour

Formed in 1997 and officially opened at Suffolk Yacht Harbour by HRH The Princess Royal in 2001, EAST is a registered charity and was established to enable adults with disabilities to enjoy the freedom and excitement of sailing on the river and at sea.

It provides suitable boats, and recruits the help it needs from able bodied people to give practical assistance and safety backup. It promotes public awareness of the needs of disabled sailors and raises funds needed by the trust to be effective in its aims.

Activities for disabled adults and their carers

Evening sailing and race training in National Squib and Paralympic Sonar keelboats from April to September including shorebased sessions and sailing on the River Orwell.

For the visually impaired, too

Introductory sailing weekends on a cruising yacht. This is also for sighted skippers considering taking visually impaired sailors on their own yacht. A week long cruise off the East Coast on a variety of cruisers, skippered by their owner.

Left: A visually impaired sailor takes the helm during one of the introductory sails

Below: Tim Reinman, (red sweater) MD of Bob Spalding Marine with EAST members after the handover of their new RIB in 2007.

In 2006 EAST launched its Vision 2012 Project to identify and train potential sailing candidates for the 2012 Paralympics. As part of the project they purchased a Sonar keelboat ('Echo' above) to provide fast and exciting sailing and, being a Paralympic class boat, the perfect way forward.

Left: Squib leaving the marina, Summer 2009.

Like all other charities EAST needs help

Any able-bodied person who is willing to give up some time to help the disabled is welcome to join EAST. Athough sailing experience is useful it is not essential. We need help in a wide range of areas: boat maintenance, fund raising and providing support on and off the water for disabled sailors.

If you are a boat owner you may be able to help by taking a disabled person along on a day sail or even a short cruise.

EAST ACTIVITES INCLUDE
- Keelboat sailing from Suffolk Yacht Harbour in our fleet of Squibs, two evenings a week from April until September
- A training programme towards RYA qualifications
- Yacht cruising weekends and a cruising week (mainly for the visually impaired)
- Racing with the Squib fleet of the Haven Ports Yacht Club.

Partners   Mr Stainless

"

One of the more recent arrivals at the yacht harbour was Mark Wingar's 'Mr Stainless' in April 2006. Mark had provided services to the yard and its businesses for years but 'Mr Stainless' is now a permanent fixture with a very smart new office and workshop at the rear of the main building.

Right: Mark Wingar always looks as bright and polished as the stainless steel itself.

Below: Curvaceous steelwork for the seats and radar arch of a Revenger 29 RIB.

The five-man team comprises himself, Tim Fox, Robin Finch, Chris Rose and Ed. Mark, Tim and Ed are mainly based at the yacht harbour while Robin and Chris work from a farm unit out at Gosbeck. Here the company produces sheet metal fabrications including boiler/water/fuel tanks, kitchens and glass balustrade handrail systems for offices etc. Mark 'floats' between the two locations wherever he is most needed.

He is a Suffolk man, through and through, who started out with a formal apprenticeship as a mechanical fitter at Cranes on the Nacton Road, Ipswich. He qualified in his final year with a course in welding and metal fabrication.

Mark started Mr Stainless in the '90s and since opening the marine division in April 2006, he's been amazed at the increased level of marine work - from the 'passing trade' generated by 550 berth-holders.

It's mostly what he calls 'tube' work, as opposed to the 'sheet' work going on at Gosbeck. Pulpits and pushpits are the stock in trade as well as radar masts, boarding ladders, liferaft carriers, sprayhood frames and just about anything you can think of made in stainless steel.

Mark's not a sailor, but a self-confessed 'petrolhead.' He does a lot of work for Revenger RIBs in Southampton and drives his own 29 ft, 60 mph, V8 inboard flyer.

Top: Revenger 29 RIB.

Above: Tim Fox (left) and Mark Wingar get to grips with fitting a new Bimini framework and sprayhood bars to a Beneteau 50.

Left: The Mr Stainless workshop at the yacht harbour produces beautiful stainless steel.

Below left: Mr Stainless works closely with the local fishing industry - here a custom cockpit guardrail on an Offshore 2000.

Bottom left: Pushpit seat on 40' yacht.

Below left: Replacement masthead fitting for S&S classic 1950s cruising yawl 'Tocatta.'

Below: Custom binnacle guard and frame for classic Excalibur 36 on which to mount 'Grand Prix' Navpod instruments.

Partners

John Gill Electrical

"

John Gill's marine electrical company has been working for Suffolk Yacht Harbour since the late '70s.

John Gill with his Shar Pei, 'Harvey'.

John Gill Electrical specialise in the installation and repair of electrical systems on yachts and motorboats including charging systems and battery management. They are professional marine electricians, fully qualified to repair, install or survey the electrical systems on most types of yacht and motor boat.

They can also survey electrical installations, design new systems and repair existing ones. They work to recognized marine industry standards on nearly all types of vessel.

The Classic Sailing Club

"

For lovers of fine classic yachts - run by enthusiasts, for enthusiasts. Jonathan Strickland and Ian Welch's Classic Sailing Club makes it possible to sail a selection of classic yachts without having the hard, skilled work of constant maintenance.

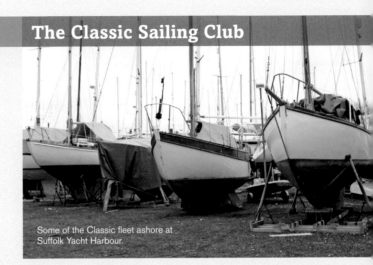

Some of the Classic fleet ashore at Suffolk Yacht Harbour.

In order to use one of the yachts as a bareboat, members must be qualified to RYA Day Skipper (bands 1-3) or RYA Coastal Skipper (Bands 4 and above). If you do not have either of the above qualifications, you can take a course on a Classic yacht.

Below: 'Hampshire Maid' is the club's superb South Coast One Design No 44, designed by Charles Nicholson and built in 1957 on the Isle of Wight by Woodnutts.

Happy Days!

I f you've ever owned a classic you'll know the feeling of dread as repair bills escalate and the guilt when fine weather means you should be working on the varnish rather than enjoying your sailing. As a member of the Classic Sailing Club, you turn up, sail, and that's it. Just concentrate on enjoying yourself!

Once you have purchased your points, the only costs for the member are the day-to-day running costs involved in using the yachts, namely diesel and other sundries. All the other costs attached to owning and operating the yachts (insurance, tax, maintenance, repair, storage, security, etc) are covered by the points . . .

The Yachts: a variety of sizes and hull types

Not only does CSC take away all the care and troubles of yacht ownership, it introduces some new pleasures too. Members have access to a variety of sizes and hull types. One day you can sail comfortably offshore using the sea kindly characteristics of one of the deep, long keeled yachts. And the next, sail in the wake of Maurice Griffiths deep into the tidal creeks of the east coast in a shallow draft, bilge keeler. Another day spend a few points day-sailing one of the smaller yachts, the next week use a few hundred taking the family on a week's cruise in a sleek, stylish 40-footer, the envy of nearly every other yachtsman.

A home for enthusiasts

The Classic Sailing Club is a home for enthusiasts, to share stories, experiences and their love for the beautiful yachts of the past. So if you haven't bought a yacht because you have no one to sail with, join the Club and they will put you in touch with others looking for crew.

Partners Eastern Electronics

"

Since 1998 Mark Wylie's company has specialised in the design and installation of very high-spec, high-tech electronic control and information systems for long-distance race yachts.

Right: Designing and installing high-tech systems into extreme raceboats is where Mark Wylie has achieved an international reputation.

Above: Mark Wylie developed the electronic systems for 'Team Concise' - the new 40 ft class which marked Pete Goss's return to long-distance singlehanded racing in the 2010 Route du Rhum, from St Malo to Guadeloupe.

Right: Mark has worked closely with Alex Thompson and his 'Hugo Boss' IMOCA class yacht in the 2010-11 Barcelona World Race and the forthcoming 2012 Vendée Globe.

Mark Wylie's company specialises in the design and installation of very high-end, high-spec electronics systems for the most sophisticated, round-the-world race yachts. This means that Mark is constantly flying round the world himself to meet up with clients' projects - like Ambition Racing's 2008/9 attempt on the Portimao Global Ocean Race for 40 ft class yachts.

As Jeremy Salvesen - *'Sweet Ambition's'* skipper commented: "Mark - Eastern Electronics - is working through a list of modifications to the communications, installing a wind turbine, lights, pumps and goodness knows what else. The man doesn't sleep, he just works away tirelessly!"

Eastern Electronics have been central to the advanced electronics systems on many of the round the world racing yacht campaigns including Team Ellen's BT Open 60 and Extreme 40 catamaran programmes.

Author/Designer

Martin Treadway

" Martin has been part of the SYH 'landscape' for over ten years, producing our regular newspaper 'Harbour Light', designing our website and brochures etc, and most recently, creating this book.

Top: Demonstrating the product on the Orwell back in the 1990s

Right: Sailing his old friend Nigel Theadom's X332 'Crikey V!' after a weekend cruise to Aldeburgh.

Below: Latest mount is this Paralympic 2.4mR singlehanded class, sailing at Frensham Pond SC, Farnham, Surrey.

Bottom: 'Editorial' vehicle on location.

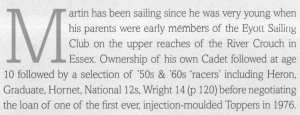

Martin has been sailing since he was very young when his parents were early members of the Eyott Sailing Club on the upper reaches of the River Crouch in Essex. Ownership of his own Cadet followed at age 10 followed by a selection of '50s & '60s 'racers' including Heron, Graduate, Hornet, National 12s, Wright 14 (p 120) before negotiating the loan of one of the first ever, injection-moulded Toppers in 1976.

This led to winning the Topper account for his fledgling advertising agency and eventually, in 1994, becoming Topper International's marketing director. This at a time when they were flat out launching an exciting new range of 'skiff-type' high performance dinghies including the ISO, Buzz, Boss, Blaze, Breeze etc and engaging in a battle royal with Laser who were following a parallel path.

Martin also knows the East Coast rivers very well having cruised them with friends from childhood and more recently in a Stella which he co-owned and rebuilt with a friend to a very high standard.

In recent years the unwelcome progress of MS has re-focussed his sailing to the RYA's Sailability programme at Frensham Pond SC near to his home in Farnham, Surrey and the new challenges of the Paralympic singlehanded class 2.4mR mini keelboat and the much simpler but very competitive Access 303 class dinghies.

17 | The Key Players | **Mike Spear**

"
Interviewed in 2009 nearly 50 years after he had the original dream, Mike reflected on a job well done and remembered some of his ingenious cost-saving schemes.

Right: Mike enjoys a joke with his grandson, Joshua Major.

Below: Where it all began. An enthusiastic young chartered surveyor from Woodbridge.

One of the most daunting problems he needed to solve in the early days was the acquisition of a dredger - capable of sucking up thousands of tons of liquid mud and depositing it several hundred yards away.

In the event, this would prove to be a project Mike solved with relish - and a considerable amount of invention. And the dredger he created - 'Muddy Boots' - remains part of the Suffolk Yacht Harbour winter landscape to this day.

Mike Spear acquired the basic dredger in early 1975 after following up an advertisement in 'Contractors Journal.' She belonged to the railway company at Stanstead Abbotts on the River Lee and came complete with half a mile of 10 inch piping in 50 ft sections. Seeing a bargain, he paid £30,000 without ever seeing it run and got a forestry transporter to ship the 100+ lengths of pipe down to Levington by road.

'Muddy Boots' is a 10 inch, cut-and-suck vessel with a massive 2 metre diameter centrifugal pump. She is powered by a 450 hp K-19, 6-cylinder Cummins diesel engine and is capable of pumping over 500 tons an hour for distribution over half a mile from source.

Nowadays 'Muddy Boots' is operated by a three-man team and her maintenance is carried out entirely 'inhouse.' In fact since 1975, just about every component part of the vessel has been replaced or reconditioned - including most of her steel hull plates.

Left: Muddy Boots at work in the winter, 'skippered' by John Butcher and Angus McWalter.

Below: Nowadays the dredged material is deposited into silt pans and designated areas of foreshore recharge.

'Finger' pontoon walkways were another obvious concern as the cost of buying new components like this was prohibitive.

Mike was exceptionally good at rooting out useful things and a breaker's yard in Newmarket produced a large quantity of secondhand Ford lorry chassis. With a bit of creative 'cutting and shutting' these formed ideal structures for the fingers.

80 ex-World War Two temporary harbour floats were sourced from builders Rogers of Felixstowe. These 8-ton flotation boxes had originally been used to support a floating barrier from Harwich to Felixstowe during the last war. They were more than adequate to support the yacht harbour's first finger pontoons.

Once again, Mike tracked down a large quantity of 70 ft long piles surplus to requirements on a development site near the local Sainsbury's. These were sawn into more practical 35 ft lengths and remain today .supporting the North wall by the Lightship.

Mike Spear receives RYA Award

In October 2003 Mike Spear was awarded a Royal Yachting Association 'Community Award.'

The Award - presented by Olympic Gold medal winner Shirley Robertson and signed by the Princess Royal - contained the inscription on the right:

IN RECOGNITION OF YOUR SERVICES TO THE WORLD OF YACHTING. ON BEHALF OF THE ASSOCIATION'S MEMBERSHIP AND ALL WHO SUPPORT ITS ACTIVITIES, THE COUNCIL OF THE ROYAL YACHTING ASSOCIATION EXPRESSES ITS DEEPEST APPRECIATION AND GRATITUDE

The Key Players   **Kim Holman**

"

Kim Holman retained his directorship and close involvement with the yacht harbour throughout his life. At the same time, he became one of the most sought after yacht designers in the world.

Yachting journalist **Peter Poland** knew him well

Right: The Stella dominated the East Coast and offshore racing scene in the '60s.

Below: Twisters. In a recent comprehensive feature on Kim Holman's designs in PBO, Peter Poland had an opportunity to sail the '60's classic in 2009: "I lounged languidly on the leeward side of the cockpit, tiller in hand, and watched as she surged to windward. No nodding; no twitchy heeling; no fuss. The effortless, long-legged power of a fast, long-keeler like a Twister is something every sailor should savour. OK, she did not accelerate (or decelerate for that matter) as quickly as a modern lightweight. But nor did she hang around. She felt as though she could go on forever, with or without my assistance. It was a delightful sensation."

I often wonder if modern sailors realise just how many great yachts came from the pen of one design office: Kim Holman and his colleagues at Holman and Pye. When Holman died in 2006 at the age of 80, a posting on a sailing website did a great job of summing up his lifetime achievements; "I believe it was said of him that he was incapable of designing an ugly boat." Of course one can ramble on ad nauseam about what makes the ideal yacht, but the saying 'what looks right is right' is invariably the conclusion. And every Holman yacht – from the humblest Stella to the biggest Admiral's Cupper – 'looked right'.

Holman grew up beside the sailing waters of the Fal and Helford River. Then during the war he joined the Royal Navy and sailed 32 ft cutters with young trainees in the choppy waters of Harwich harbour while stationed at HMS Ganges. This was followed by a spell in the Mediterranean before he returned to Blighty where, based on the Humber, he became the youngest officer to run a minesweeper. Then, when the war ended, he went West again - to Bristol University - where he said he "didn't get a degree but did learn to drink and have fun."

So - duly degree-less - Holman found his way back to the East Coast, where he joined yacht designer Jack Jones at Waldringfield and embarked on a long and successful career. And *Phialle* - one of his earliest 'solo' efforts, which he designed for himself and raced in 1956 – was the first of many winners.

Holman then moved to West Mersea and bought a share in Gowens sailmakers; and set to work designing a succession of successful yachts that were to hoist Gowens sails. These were invariably designed to the old RORC handicap rule, which produced yachts that were as happy racing offshore as they were family cruising. This was the era of the true cruiser-racer, and artists such as Holman, Buchanan, Raymond Wall and Rod Stephens drew beautiful yachts that sailed superbly and looked sublime. None of these RORC generation yachts had broad beam saloons, cavernous aft cabins secreted beneath wide sterns or palatial shower cubicles; unlike today's AWB's (average white blobs). But I don't really care. They were proper yachts.

As the years moved on, Holman designed a seemingly endless procession of 'winners'; yachts that sailed as well as they looked. The ubiquitous Stella, aimed to be a more commodious development of the Folkboat, took off in the early '60s and was one of the first 'production family cruiser-racers' ever built – albeit in wood, not GRP. Then – when fibreglass took over – Holman developed his hugely successful one-off *Twister of Mersea* into the Twister production yacht; built in large numbers by his brother Jack down at Uphams in Brixham. And at much the same time, he demonstrated his versatility by drawing Admirals Cup winners such as the mighty *Fanfare*.

Holman was also an original director and shareholder at SYH. He was not as 'hands on' as some of the founding directors but was always very supportive. What's more, his name as a famous and successful yacht designer gave a degree of 'gravitas' to the company; especially in the early years when the harbour was evolving from a muddy hole into a smart marina. He moored his Hustler 35, *Jemina A* at SYH from the mid 1980s to the mid 1990s and was a director up to his death. His two nieces retain a small Holman family interest in SYH. Kim is especially remembered for his sense of humour and dry wit, which made any gathering, business or social meeting great fun for all concerned. He was a charming man, enjoyed the good things in life and his generous spirit influenced all who came into contact with him.

It would take several pages to list all of Holman's great designs; and I suspect that sailors based at SYH will know most of them anyway. Suffice it to say that from the French Wauquiez yard's Centurion, Gladiateur and Amphitrite models to the early Hustlers and Elizabethans to the plethora of Oysters, every Holman designed production yacht did its job superbly. What's more, they all remain near the top of most sensible sailors' shopping lists when they are searching for a new brokerage yacht.

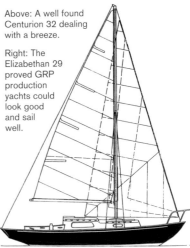

Above: A well found Centurion 32 dealing with a breeze.

Right: The Elizabethan 29 proved GRP production yachts could look good and sail well.

Above: The Rustler 36 is a once-in-a-lifetime indulgence in something that is very beautiful, very practical and very seaworthy.

Below: The HP46 was the first Oyster Deck Saloon yacht, beginning a trend that would revolutionize cruising yacht design.

" . . . he was incapable of designing an ugly boat . . .

The Key Players   **Eric Wright**

> Eric's successful Ipswich company, Wright & Sons (Ipswich) Ltd, built traditional clinker sailing dinghies in oak and mahogany at a time when the 'plywood revolution' had already arrived in strength. But there remained a strong market for his pretty 'Twinkle 10 & 12' and sportier 'Family 14.' Eric was approached for his opinion of the Suffolk Yacht Harbour project and invited to invest in it. He remained on the board until his death in 2008 at the age of 92.

The Family Fourteen was beautifully built and was much lighter than it looked, with a surprisingly good turn of speed.

When Eric was approached in 1967 for his opinion and possibly some capital, he was at 55 the oldest member of the working group. He and his father had been producing small wooden rowing and sailing dinghies from premises in Ipswich since the First World War. But his son, stepping out of the Wright tradition, upped sticks and sought a new life in New Zealand. His two daughters opted for Canada.

Wright and Sons were left without an heir, so the head of the business began to sink his enthusiasm elsewhere - into the glutinous mud of the River Orwell and the embryo Suffolk Yacht Harbour.

Wheels were set in motion and the triumvirate marched on the dreaded planners, applying for permission for a 'yacht harbour' for 600 boats on the 36 acre site.

It took the addition of Ipswich architect John Adams to add his weight and expertise to the application for the result to be achieved and he was incorporated on to the board.

The **Twinkle Twelve** and the **Twinkle Ten** were built by Wright & Sons (Ipswich) Ltd in the '50s, '60s and '70s from Mahogany on oak frames. Wrights also built a 14-footer known as the **Family Fourteen**. The Twelves were 12ft (3.66m) overall and 4'8 (1.42) in beam. They carried about 80sq ft (7.4sq m) of sail - originally on gunter rigs which have been largely or wholly replaced by bermudan. The home of the Twinkle Twelve is the Overy Staithe Sailing Club where there are 25 - 30 Twinkle 12s and a small number of 10s and 14s. These charming boats are widespread but the only known active fleet is at Burnham Overy Staithe, Norfolk.

Below: During production of this book, Eric Wright's nephew Peter Wright, kindly produced this photograph of his 'as new' Family Fourteen which he acquired on the internet in 2008. He keeps her on a mooring in Burnham on Crouch.

Peter Wright is on the current board of Suffolk Yacht Harbour.

A Family Fourteen sailing on the Colne at Wivenhoe in 1975.

On this page: Overy Staithe Sailing club in North Norfolk still has a good fleet of Wright-built Twinkle Tens, Twelves and Family Fourteens racing on their breezy, tidal waters.

Pictures on this page reproduced with the kind permission of the Overy Staithe Sailing Club, North Norfolk.

The Key Players

Geoffrey Ambrose Hubbard

"

Geoff Hubbard, a local refrigeration engineer, was invited to join the new board of directors for his impressive financial skill and enviable business experience.

Geoff also put himself and his boat *Irene of Boston* to work on a seven month fact-finding voyage of European marinas.

Below: The trainer Ferdy Murphy had a successful partnership with Geoff until the mid '90s when Hubbard became the largest permit holder in the country, owning and training his own horses.

Geoff trained and qualified as an electrical engineer and served his time during the Second World War with the Royal Engineers. He married Marjorie Cooper in April 1942 and they had two daughters, Sandra and Janet. He and his father, Percy, set up Suffolk Auto Electrical Services in 1946 in Saxmundham. His business credentials were soon in evidence when he rented 200 of the first TV sets to the Woodbridge US Airbase.

Geoff soon became a conspicuously successful local business-man and was invited to join the new SYH board. He was one of the co-founders of Anglia Television and quickly built companies into major forces in the refrigeration industry. G A H Refrigeration in Woodbridge, today remains one of the most respected suppliers of refrigerated vehicles to the industry.

" he liked his horses big and black . . .

Below: Geoff Hubbard receives the Hennessy Cognac Gold Cup at Newbury, won by his 40 to 1 outsider 'Sibton Abbey' in November 1992. The 'Hennessy' is run over a distance of 3 miles, 2 1/2 furlongs over 21 fences.

Throughout his years on the board, Geoff's successful businesses and financial expertise steered the yacht harbour safely through some stormy waters. He was a real enthusiast for the marina and carried out his own fact-finding cruise in 1970, visiting every marina between Suffolk and Majorca and putting over 4,000 miles under his keel. He brought back a rich stock of data and photographs that were to provide vital information for years to come.

In the 1980s, Geoff Hubbard began investing heavily in the Sport of Kings and over the next 30 years the Hubbard emerald green and white silks became one of the most successful racing stables in the country. There were endless successes - from *Shady Deal* winning the Whitbread Gold Cup in 1981 to *Sibton Abbey's* 40-1 shock win over favourite *Jodami* in the 1992 Hennessey Gold Cup.

"Geoff always used to say to me that he liked his horses big and black," said trainer Ferdy Murphy, once assistant to the Suffolk-based owner-trainer.

Geoff Hubbard died early in the year 2000. Since then slowly, but sadly, the familiar sight of the emerald green and white silks that had carried the Hubbard identity for more than 30 years are finally becoming a rarity on British racecourses.

Below Geoff and Eric Wright getting 'down and dirty' in the early days of construction.

Above left: Geoff's father, Percy William Ambrose Hubbard worked for Brooke Marine in Lowestoft, and raced their powerboats in many prestigious events around Europe. In April 1912, he competed in 'The International Meeting de Canots Automobiles' at The Sporting Club de Monaco, winning the coveted Cordon Rouge.

Left: Geoff and Marjorie out 'on the town.'

The Key Players

Chris Carter Jonas

"
Born in Hitchin, Herts, Chris was a partner of the London chartered surveyors, Carter Jonas & Sons.

He had a deep fascination with the yacht harbour project and designed much of the plant used in its construction.

Sadly, Chris died in Ipswich in 1980, at the age of 53, after a short battle with cancer.

CARTER JONAS

Carter Jonas was founded in 1855, when John Carter Jonas set himself up as an auctioneer in Cambridge.

The firm's estate-management business started when the future Marquess of Lincolnshire appointed John Carter Jonas to run his family estates in Buckinghamshire, and Carter Jonas's extensive association with Oxbridge colleges was expanded when the firm took over Castle, Field & Castle in Oxford in 1924.

The firm strengthened its estate management business during the war years, when it managed many estates whose staff were serving in the armed forces. Carter Jonas remained a family firm until 1965, when the Partnership was enlarged to include senior members of staff.

By 2009 there were 20 offices, notably strengthened by the acquisition of three Egertons offices in the Capital.

Chris was born in 1927, schooled at Charterhouse and continued his education at Peterhouse, Cambridge where he read engineering. He had just escaped conscription during the War but was passionate about aircraft and was commissioned into the RAF in 1948 as a Flight Lieutenant.

He excelled as a pilot and graduated to the Empire Test Pilot School at RAF Farnborough in 1952. Two years later he retired from the RAF to join Rolls Royce at Hucknall as a full time test pilot, working on the development of the original ejector seat and the 'Flying Bedstead' - the infamous and extremely dangerous forerunner to the VTOL Harrier 'Jump Jet.' In his time with the RAF, Rolls Royce and after 1958, BOAC, he flew no less than 90 aircraft, including a period flying long haul with BOAC.

He had married Eve Anson in 1954 who he met dinghy sailing in Lymington - another passion carried over from boyhood sailing trips with his parents on the Norfolk Broads.

His second career began in 1959 when he returned to

Chris at Orford Quay, Suffolk.

Left: The Victorian gaff cutter 'Leila' which Chris co-owned with his brother Harry. 'Leila' was a rare example of a Victorian racing cutter, built in 1892 in Charlton, London for a businessman who sailed with the Royal Temple Yacht Club at Ramsgate. She won the Round Britain race in 1904.

Cambridge to devote two years reading Estate Management and preparing for taking on the family firm, Carter Jonas. He and Eve moved to Ipswich in 1961 where he started working in the local office, becoming a partner in 1964, sharing his time with the Ipswich and London offices.

In 1967 he was introduced to the yacht harbour project and as was typical of the man, threw himself into it with real gusto. His engineering skill and 'hands-on' abilities enabled Chris to produce engineering calculations and drawings for much of the construction plant that kept the project moving forward through the trickiest times.

Above: Chris and Eve sailing their 505 racing dinghy on the Lymington River.

He remained loyal to his flying background, acquiring a Cessna 172 as a company aeroplane. This was later upgraded to a Helio Super Courier, an aircraft with a formidable 'short field' performance in which Chris was able to deliver Partners of the family firm into sites 'off the beaten track.'

Sailing was also a major part of Chris's fascinating, but sadly short life. From 1959-62 he shared a 15 ton, Victorian racing gaff cutter called *Leila* with his brother Harry and in the 60s and 70s raced a trio of yachts called *Zeelust I, II,* and *III* - a Fortunella 34, and a Van de Stadt Rebel 41 and an Oyster 39.

Below: A Helio H-395 Super Courier aircraft similar to the one owned by Chris Carter Jonas from 1959-62. Around 500 of these aircraft were manufactured in Pittsburg, Kansas between 1954 and 1974. They had a great 'short field' capability and - in skilled hands - could fly without stalling down to below 30mph! These characteristics ensured the Helios played an important role in the Vietnam war.

He became a serious and able racing yachtsman and a member of the Royal Ocean Racing Club to which he became Honorary Surveyor in 1973, spending a year negotiating with London Transport who, while boring a new underground line underneath RORC Headquarters off St James's, almost demolished the building!

Chris was a founder member of the Haven Ports Yacht Club and involved with the organisation of their many championships. He also enjoyed membership of the Royal Harwich YC (ex rear commodore), the RYA, Carthusian YC, Waldringfield SC and EAORA (ex committee).

Chris in the Cessna 172 with his children Tink and Trish.

Below: Eve Carter Jonas

John Adams

"
John, who died in September 2005 at the age of 89, had many admirable qualities. But he will be most fondly remembered for his kindness and unique sense of humour.

John Adams, Architectural projects.

• Total rebuild of Alston's Factory

• Development of Volvo Car Depot

• Nardin & Peacock

• Major alterations to Waldringfield Sailing Club (probably 1970s)

• Numerous projects for his friends Sue Ryder and Leonard Cheshire

• Projects for Thorpeness Estates Ltd

• One of his proudest projects was a toilet block in Wardown Park, Luton which had the distinction of being his first ever solo contract.

• By coincidence, his last contract was the toilet block at SYH !

John Treadwell Adams was born on 29 May 1916 at Addington near Buckingham, where his parents had a farm. He qualified as an Assistant Architect in 1939, and was employed by Huntingdon Council. In the same year, a few months before the outbreak of war, he married Norah on 1st June.

As a 23 year old he was called up and served with the Royal Engineers during hostilities.

His interests were cricket, football, flying, sailing, cars and golf. He founded the Pheasant Pluckers Golfing Society in the 1960s, for which qualification was a very low aptitude for the game. He was maybe one of the very few golfers who have broken a leg while performing a swing. His leg slipped on the turf (he was usually in a bunker) and after a resounding 'crack' his golfing partners carried the casualty off to the clubhouse on an old door prior to driving John to hospital. There was an ambulance strike on at the time! He did not suffer in silence according to reliable witnesses. The Society still exists but is more respectably now known as simply The Pheasant Golfing Society.

John's real passion in life was his 1935 Hornet Moth biplane which he owned during the 1960s and hangared at Ipswich airfield. G - ADLY is still flying - most recently in 2007 - to Perth in Scotland, in the commercial ownership of a Petroleum Aviation company.

Stephen Rendle photo

John's chunky little de Havilland DH 87B Hornet Moth G-ADLY, photographed at the Badminton Air Day, in 1990. She was built in 1935.

John's navigation did not inspire confidence if you were the poor sod in the passenger seat! His 'trick' for finding Ipswich when lost - he usually was - was to find the coast and follow it until Felixstowe pier came into view - then follow the railway line inland and, lo and behold, Ipswich should appear! The one flaw to this 'solution' was knowing whether to turn left or right when the coastline was encountered . . .

John's son Robin has inherited the commitment of the first generation 'activists' and sits on the current board of directors.

" . . . if you were the poor sod in the passenger seat!

Right: Peter Phillips, keeping a weather eye on the harbour.

Peter Phillips

❝

Peter was a master of logistics and accounting systems and established the yacht harbour chandlery as major profit centre for the business. He was skillfully assisted in this process by the remarkable Una Jenkins.

In spite of his engineering background, Peter had a love of 'messing about on the river' in his Norwegian - styled fishing boat. But there was certainly no 'messing' about Peter's disciplined and practical approach to organising the harbour and turning into an efficient and, more importantly, profitable operation. He established the Chandlery as a comprehensive profit centre and continued to apply his high standards throughout the business. He was a master of logistics and accounts, ably assisted for many years by the remarkable Una Jenkins, a stalwart book-keeper who converted the office from its ageing 'Kalamazoo' rotational card index systems to a thoroughly up-to-date computer network.

Peter retired in the late '80s to spend more time travelling the world with his wife Joan. He had gained an heir-apparent in the shape of Jonathan Dyke who took over as Harbour Master in 1987.

Peter Phillips died in 1996.

Right: The remarkable **Una Jenkins** who modernised the office accounting systems in the '70s.

Charles Stennett

❝

Charles owned the land on which Suffolk Yacht Harbour was built. It had become degraded and unsuitable for arable use following the breach of the seawall in 1942.

He was a real Suffolk character and while he shared Mike Spear's vision to turn the land into a yacht harbour, he was concerned about the 'large muddy hole' owned by the bank! But he did provide valuable earth-moving machinery in the early days. Sadly, Charles died prematurely in 1979.

His wife Wendy continues to take an interest in the yacht harbour and his son Mark is on the current board of directors.

Right: Charles with his wife Wendy, at a local gymkhana.

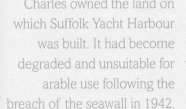

The Key Players   Jonathan Dyke

"

Jonathan has been a 'hands on' director of the yacht harbour for 26 years and its managing director since 2001. Although too young to remember much about the 'mudlarking' antics of the 1960s, as a director he has played a leading role in all the major developments of recent years which have fully refined the harbour into a facility that bears comparison with the very best marinas in Northern Europe.

Above: Jonathan's West Solent One-Design W30 'Benita' in pre-start monoeuvres with another WS at a SYH Classic Regatta.

Jonathan grew up in Cambridge and travelled to Brightlingsea to satisfy his lust for dinghy sailing – initially in a Leader dinghy – a design from the '60s that looked and performed very much like a smaller Wayfarer.

His father was a keen East Coast sailor, too with an interesting selection of small cruiser-racers including a Tomahawk, Pandora and Verle 900, which formed Jonathan's grounding in bigger boats.

After leaving school, he managed to win a place at Southampton Institute on their highly respected Yacht & Boatyard Management course. Boats were in his blood and he threw himself into his studies - as well as finding himself working on 'release' throughout the course at some interesting south coast boatyards.

He qualified in 1979 at the age of 22, and embarked on an intensive hands-on learning curve with some legendary boatyards: A spell in Norfolk with Jack Powells in Wroxham (Offshore Yachts) putting together the successful Halcyon 23 and 27 range and the never-to-be-forgotten Nantucket Clipper 31, designed by Alan Buchanan.

He then headed south to Lymington to work in Berthon's highly sophisticated and technical drawing office on projects such as a

GRP 'landing craft' for the Sheik of Qatar. This ex military vessel housed two beach buggies and three Harley-Davidsons to keep the occupants amused. At Berthon he also worked on the mighty *Heath's Condor* - the 78 ft moulded mahogany maxi that had been the hot favourite for the second Whitbread Round the World Race in 1977-78. She was skippered by Robin Knox-Johnston and Lesley Williams but sadly lost her revolutionary, part carbon, 100 ft mast - ruining her chances.

Jonathan then headed east to Suffolk for a two year spell designing rigs at the Anchor Mill drawing office of Lee Ward Rigging near Pinmill, followed by a hectic year at Colvic who were then pumping out in excess of 2,000 mouldings a year!

In 1982, he took a telephone call from family friend Mike Spear, who invited him down 'for a chat' on the Lightship to see if he fancied helping out harbour manager David Lewis. He agreed, but was quickly and unexpectedly 'fast-tracked' to manager by David's premature death – leading to a steep learning curve with much responsibility at the age of 25.

Three years later, he became the youngest member of the Board and with the retirement of the then harbour master, Peter Phillips in 1987, he took on that role, too.

Jonathan's own love of boats, particularly classic yachts, began in earnest with the acquisition of an old Rowhedge Ironworks-built Stella at about this time, which he spent happy times restoring. (with the useful back-up of his 'own' boatyard in support!)

The Stella was followed by the badly dilapidated West Solent One Design, *Benita* W30 designed by H. G. May and built by Berthon in 1931. The stunningly beautiful WSOD has, like the more modern Stella, enjoyed a strong resurgence of interest in the last 20 years. *Benita* W30 was trucked back to Suffolk and fastidiously restored prior to a distinguished racing career, winning trophies including the priceless Queenborough Bowl at Aldeburgh Yacht Club.

Above: Jonathan's striking Mystery class 39 ft classic 'Cereste' going upwind 'like a witch . . .'

. . . and (below) she's not too shabby off the wind either! Pictured here at the Panerai Cowes Regatta in July, 2010. 'Cereste' also won the prestigious British Classic Yacht Club Regatta on two previous occasions.

Left: His first wooden boat was a Stella, which celebrated its 50th anniversary at the 2009 SYH Classic Regatta and turned out a superb fleet of 17.

Jonathan Dyke

Benita continues to perform well in the Classic Regattas in the hands of her current owner, William McLeod Scott.

In 1997 Jonathan acquired *Cereste,* the gorgeous Mystery Class 39 which he still owns and cherishes today. Originally built in 1938 by the Shoreham Yacht Works from mahogany on oak frames, she had actually started life as a masthead cutter. A three year restoration was carried out at the yard where she was converted to a three-quarter rigged sloop, transforming her performance. One of the first passages in her new guise was down to the Solent to follow the 2001 America's Cup Jubilee Regatta and it was here that Jonathan first thought of the idea for an East Coast Classic regatta based at the Yacht Harbour.

When the chairman, Eric Wright retired in 2001, Mike Spear took the chair and Jonathan was appointed Managing Director, a position he continues to hold today and his many achievements in the last ten years are already covered in detail earlier in this book.

He has an interesting way of articulating the company's success: "It is where it is today because it is not a family business..

It is a business of families."

Above: 'Cruising on 'Cereste'.

Below: The familiar sight of Jonathan's 39' Mystery class 'Cereste' motoring back into the marina after the 2009 regatta.

Maurice Moss

"

Maurice Moss, our company secretary, provided sterling support for the the yacht harbour in the 16 year period of dramatic growth between 1985 and 2001.

In spite of knowing very little about boats - or even yacht harbours - Maurice transformed the office administration, including the establishment of the first fully integrated computer system for running the company's accounts and credit control.

Maurice was a lover of steam and a serious railway 'aficianado', who devoted his leisure time to the magnificent model railway layout in his home loft.

John Butcher

"

John Butcher has tirelessly operated our dredger 'Muddy Boots' for 40 years - vitally keeping the marina free of silt and mud for berth-holders.

Right: John 'Whiskers' Butcher who worked alongside Noel Dennis who also drove the dredger, 'Muddy Boots.'

A 'lovable rogue' is a description often applied to John Butcher who has been gracing the yacht harbour as long as anyone can remember. He's never been a full time employee, but has operated the dredger 'Muddy Boots' every winter for forty years - recently assisted by Angus McWalter, an HGV driver who returned to the yacht harbour in 2008 having been a shipwright/boatbuilder here in the '80s and '90s (p.82).

John - more commonly know as 'Whiskas' - is a City & Guilds shipwright, trained by Priors of Burnham-on-Crouch in the '60s. He then joined the inshore fishing industry, specialising in the rich eel harvest available on the River Orwell every summer.

New generations . . .

It has been very rewarding to see new generations of the original founding families spending time working at the yacht harbour during summer school or university holidays. Eric Wright's two grandsons, Christopher and Graham, worked at SYH during 1998 and 1999. Daniel Adams, John Adams' grandson spent time making himself useful during the mid 1990s while James and Harry Carter-Jonas, Chris Carter Jonas's grandsons helped out during the summers of 2009 and 2010.

Right: John and Sarah Carter Jonas off the marina in their Oyster 26, 'Zeelust IV'.

18   The Board of Directors in 2010

Mike Spear   Jonathan Dyke

Robin Adams

Mark Stennett

The seven occupants of the seats on the main board of directors in 2011 are all, with the exception of Jonathan Dyke, part of or descendants of the original 'gang' whose inspiration and vision got the project off the ground in the '60s. Of that illustrious group, only **Mike Spear** remains with us and actively involved in the running of the yacht harbour (see p.116).

Jonathan Dyke, the current Managing Director has been at the yacht harbour for 29 years, a director for 25 years and the MD since 2001. His full profile starts on page 128.

Robin Adams is the son of architect John Adams (p.126). He has a keen interest in historic and classic cars, owns a Morgan and regularly attends the Goodwood Revival and Festival of Speed meetings. He has interests in property and spent his working life with his father in his architectural practice and as a result drew virtually all the plans for the early harbour development and buildings. He likes to travel as much and when ever is possible.

Mark Stennett has inherited his father Charles' expertise and enthusiasm for custom built plant and machinery and continues to help onsite with maintenance. He worked in the Yacht Harbour workshops while at school as a teenager, when he developed a particular interest in plant and equipment. He likes to be involved in plant acquisition and planning and from time to time gets involved in engineering projects. He recently built a snow plough attachment for the SYH four wheel drive tractor to deal with the difficult winters we now seem to be experiencing! Mark lives in Levington with his Thai partner, Lat and daughters Rebecca and Katrina. He also has a high speed RIB which he uses for skiing and fishing. Often he will be seen driving around the harbour in the evening performing an informal security duty. He holds an HGV licence and often drives the length and breadth of the country, contracted to various hauliers.

John Carter Jonas is the son of founding director Chris Carter Jonas (p.124). He was educated at Gordonstoun School, Moray in Scotland before embarking on a marine industry career at the (then) Anglian Training Boatbuilding Centre at Oulton Broad, Lowestoft. This was followed by fourteen years with Landamores in Wroxham, including a two year boatbuilding apprenticeship, and then more solid study for three years at Southampton College on their legendary Yacht & Boatyard Management course. He then reinforced all the learning with three more years of paid employment as an assistant production manager at Landamores.

In 1987 he headed to the Orwell to begin a long spell with Fox's in Ipswich where he remains as Marina Manager.

He and his wife Sarah continue to enjoy a deep interest in sailing with their Oyster 26, *Zeelust IV* which is berthed here at Suffolk Yacht Harbour. They have two children - James, 18 and Harry, 16. John's non-sailing interests include golf, playing saxophone and messing about with old Land Rovers.

We are especially grateful to Sarah for her help with historical details of the early days and the loan of precious photographs of the project and its protagonists.

Peter Wright is the grandson of Gary Wright, the founder of Wright & Sons (Ipswich) Ltd and nephew to Eric Wright, one of the original shareholders of Suffolk Yacht Harbour, (p.120).

Educated at Ipswich School and Caius, Cambridge where he graduated with an MA in Engineering, he became a Fellow of the Institute of Nuclear Engineers, a Member of the Institute of Mechanical Engineers and a Member of the Institute of Electrical Engineers. He worked in power generation, mostly nuclear, from 1972 to 2005, including periods in Spain and the US. He established Wright Outcomes Ltd., a nuclear energy consultancy, in 2005 with clients in the UK, Czech Republic, China, Pakistan and the International Atomic Energy Agency in Vienna.

Peter was also a great help in the production of this book with details of the Wright family and the clinker dinghies the company built - the 'Twinkle 10', 'Twinkle 12' and 'Family Fourteen'.

John Carter Jonas

Research also led the book's Editor to the very helpful members of Burnham Overy Staithe Sailing Club in north Norfolk where a considerable fleet of 'Eric's boats' still enjoy fleet racing. Peter himself has recently managed to acquire an immaculate Family Fourteen (p.121) from this club, which he sails from his home 'port' of Burnham on Crouch, Essex. He also part owns a Moody 425 *Wild Thyme* which has recently arrived at SYH.

Peter has two children, Christopher and Claire and there are three Grandchildren. He re-married in 2005 to Marta Nedvedicka.

He has been a shareholder of the yacht harbour since 1974 and a director since 2002. He is Hon. Treasurer and a Director of The Crouch YC, Burnham.

Nicky Major is Mike Spear's daughter and mother of Joshua Major who is now also also forging a career with Suffolk Yacht Harbour (p. 78).

Peter Wright

Nicky Major

Nicky had an early love of sailing, spending happy times racing Cadets at Waldringfield SC and on the open meeting circuit. She also crewed in dinghy star David East's National 12, as well as helming in Fireflies and Squibs. She learned about keelboat sailing on her father's Holman & Pye designed 31ft yacht, *Maleni* - which was very similar to a big 'Twister'.

Nicky married Alan Major and together they raced the family SS34 *Voile d'Or* - a sister ship to Ted Heath's *Morning Cloud*.

They now own the Swan 41 *Moustique* which they campaign at the Swan European Regatta as well as enjoying her as a much loved family cruising boat. Nicky also devotes much of her time supporting her daughter Jessica's competitive riding and eventing on a programme that includes the Horse of the Year Show, Royal International and Burghley.

Below: The pretty waterfront at Wivenhoe on the River Colne on a busy summer evening.

Suffolk Yacht Harbour is uniquely located on the beautiful River Orwell to take advantage of its proximity to all the other East Coast rivers:

The Deben and Alde to the north with the Rivers Stour Blackwater, Colne and Crouch to the south.

A little further afield lies the mighty Thames estuary and the River Medway.

The East Coast Rivers were first brought to the attention of cruising yachtsmen in the 1920s by the writings of Maurice Griffiths, editor of *Yachting Monthly* for 40 years and author of the classic work *The Magic of the Swatchways* which remains in print today.

Mr Griffiths followed this up with many more books on these rivers and his regular features on cruising the east coast in the magazine inspired a new band of yachtsmen. Such was the interest that British Railways laid on special 'weekend cruising' tickets which allowed sailors to catch an early Friday evening train from Liverpool Street to any number of little east coast 'ports' - e.g. Maldon, Wivenhoe, Burnham-on-Crouch. They could then sail on to another harbour and return to London on the same ticket. Remember this was long before Beeching had closed down hundreds of miles of coast bound tracks and stations in 1963 when even little Maldon had two stations, Maldon East and Maldon North!

Nowadays of course, this part of coastal Britain retains all its charm and offers sailors a wonderful choice of cruising destinations - as well as the unique, east coast navigational challenge of tides, swatchways and mudbanks. With careful planning, all the destinations shown on these two pages are reachable in a day's sail from Levington in the average 25-35 ft cruising boat. Many are even available to visit and return from on the same day. Nor do you have to head downstream. Our own beautiful River Orwell has much to see and linger over. The 'Butt & Oyster' at Pinmill, arguably the east coast's most famous waterside inn and anchorage, makes an ideal lunch destination if you only have a few hours.

As well as local cruising, Suffolk Yacht Harbour is the perfect 'departure' point for crossing the North Sea - in particular to experience the delights of Holland and her inland waterway system. There are a number of entry points into the country either in the south via Flushing or Vlissingen - which offer a shorter sea passage - or via Ijmuiden in the north into the North Sea Canal taking in Amsterdam and the Isselmeer.

The Ramsholt Arms is one of the River Deben's favourite watering holes.

Above centre: The iconic, art deco Royal Corinthian Yacht Club building at Burnham on Crouch.

Above: The ancient Tidemill at Woodbridge conceals a fine, modern marina for 200 yachts.

Below: The lovely Georgian waterfront at Burnham-on-Crouch.

Far left: A gaff cutter about to bring up in the river at Aldeburgh.

Left: Two oyster smacks enter the lock at Heybridge Basin on the River Blackwater.

Right: A fleet of Loch Long One Designs racing up the river at Aldeburgh.

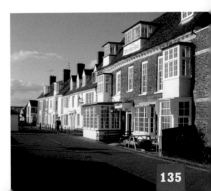

135

Below: Aerial photograph taken on 5th June
2010, soon after the roof was clad.

20

2011. A yacht harbour for the future.

A major expansion to our
headquarters took place in
2010 with the construction
of **The Harbour Centre,**
an exciting new building
designed by the Wincer
Kievenaar Partnership.

In 2009, an approach was made to our award-winning architects, Wincer Kievenaar, to design an 'iconic' new office/administration building on the same site as our existing facility. A severe absence of space and up-to-date facilities necessitated this modernisation/expansion which had been on the drawing board for some time.

It would need to encompass the existing chandlery and provide a range of offices, meeting rooms and storage to future-proof our requirements for the next 15-20 years. Importantly, the building should develop and expand the unique style of finish the architects had set in motion with the Harbour Room and new Spalding showroom. By careful planning, the chandlery was able to stay open throughout the re-build, this being the only major part of the existing building which was retained.

Above: Demolition of the old buildings took
place very rapidly in December 2009.

Right: The sheer scale of the new structure
could now be fully appreciated - May 2010.

Because of the relatively poor ground conditions, the architects decided on deep piling, tied with a ring beam to support the steel frame structure which they had specified. The whole building was designed in an environmentally-friendly way.

The revolutionary Eco under-floor heating and hot water system uses seawater drawn from the harbour which passes through heat exchangers and a source pump system to produce hot water at virtually no cost! This is the first UK marina to incorporate this advanced technology and has produced a building which is virtually carbon neutral.

The striking design is characterised by the generous use of Siberian larch cladding, incorporating 'solar finning' - horizontally mounted rows of thin planks which create shading within the large areas of glass, like fixed venetian blinds, keeping the inside cool in summer and warm in winter. This is enhanced by high insulation qualities and modern double glazing throughout.

The new build features multiple access points, with total step-free accessibility on the ground floor. The architects have been careful to create interesting shapes and angles to avoid any feel of a plain, slab-sided structure. There is generous use of stainless steel, outside terraces and external spiral staircases.

Above: The larch cladding is attached with stainless steel screws which are each individually counter-bored and plugged with larch dowels. Over time the colour of this untreated timber will soften to a silvery grey.

Below: Beautiful stainless steel posts and rails on the impressive central staircase by Mr Stainless. Welded construction has been used to connect component parts which shows how marine techniques transfer seamlessly to non-marine fabrications.

Above: Another aerial photo from June 2010 showing how well the new building settles into its surroundings.

Right: Balconies and balustrades provide outdoor space to much of the upper floors and views across the site.

Below right: The Chandlery and main entrance have ramped access to the building's ground floor areas.

Below: Harwich Harbour monitors traffic with the new radar scanner.

The low-pitched roofs have a decidedly 'Alpine' quality while the membrane sheet covering is virtually indestructable.

Three storeys.

The main south easterly elevation still looks out over the East Harbour and at three storeys high, is very impressive.

The main entrance is via double glazed doors leading to a reception area with staff access to the chandlery and a stunning

Above: Siberian larch cladding.

Left: The existing partner buildings are of high quality and designed in a way that facilitates enlargement when needs arise.

Below. Finished on schedule, looking beautiful and occupied early in December, 2010. The Harbour Centre was officially opened by Griff Rhys-Jones on Easter Saturday, 23 April 2011.

Below: A grand entrance

stainless, curved staircase to the first floor offices and other facilities. The first floor has much improved accommodation for accounts, administration and the marina and harbour master's offices. There are wide, panoramic views over the marina and River Orwell from the upper floors and balconies.

When viewed back from the river the architecture aims to be visually diverse and 'sits' nicely under the hill where the varied gables and external staircases have produced a distinguised new 'landmark' building.

The revolutionary Eco under-floor heating and hot water system uses seawater drawn from the harbour which passes through heat exchangers and a source pump system to produce hot water at virtually no cost! We are the first UK marina to incorporate this advanced technology.

The Harbour Centre is disabled friendly with ramped access and offers all the associated facilities. It has excellent offices and meeting rooms and is CAT 5 cabled to enable the easy installation of modern communication, computer, video and technology systems. All set amongst spectacular views and enjoying the most stunning marine surroundings in the heart of this busy marina.

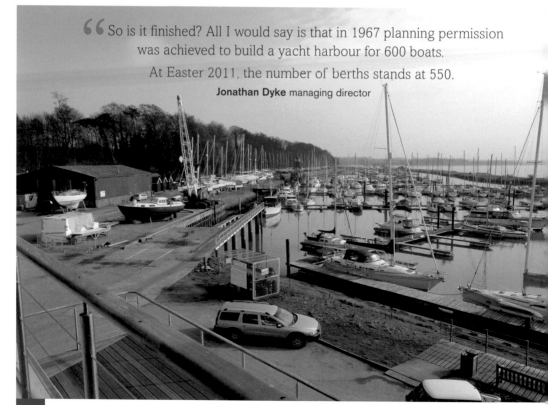

❝ So is it finished? All I would say is that in 1967 planning permission was achieved to build a yacht harbour for 600 boats.
At Easter 2011, the number of berths stands at 550.

Jonathan Dyke managing director

Acknowledgements

Over the course of the last 45 years, Suffolk Yacht Harbour owes a deep debt of gratitude to a great number of its friends and partners, without whose support and patience this enterprise would never have been the success it has.

It would be impossible to name them all, but a few that stand out are listed here.

We can only apologise to the hundreds of others.

- Wincer Kievenaar Partnership

- The Landscape Partnership

- Ensors Chartered Accountants.

- Blocks Solicitors

- The British Marine Federation

- The Yacht Harbour Association

- British Petroleum

- Don Chadwick

- Bob Curle

- Joe Arbon

- Gordon Burns

- Len Tuckwell

- Leslie Carter

- Dick Fox

- Alan Troop

- Geoff Burrell

- Mike Pawsey

- John Watson

- AE (Dicky) Bird

- Mike Stone

The layout and facilities at the yacht harbour are continually improving so this plan is a 'moment in time' in early 2011.

Facilities

ST	Showers/Toilet
LY	Laundry
WS	Workshop
MM	Mini-Market
HO	Harbour Office
HPYC	Haven Ports YC

Onsite Businesses

ES	East Anglian Sea School
CC	Clarke & Carter Interyacht
RJ	R&J Marine Electronics
FM	French Marine Motors
QS	Quantum Sails GBR
RM	Rig Magic
ET	East Anglian Sailing Trust
BSM	Bob Spalding Marine
CS	Classic Sailing Club
MS	Mr Stainless

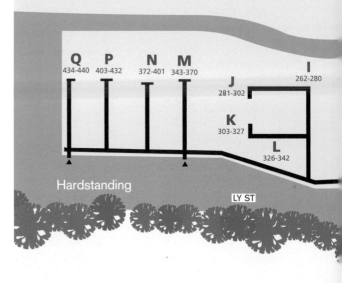

Q 434-440 P 403-432 N 372-401 M 343-370 J 281-302 I 262-280 K 303-327 L 326-342

Hardstanding

LY ST